The Lundy Granite Company

An Industrial Adventure

PETER ROTHWELL
&
MYRTLE TERNSTROM

Westwell Publishing
DEVON

First published 2008
Westwell Publishers
41 Bude Street
Appledore
Devon
EX39 1PS

isbn   (10) 0-9521413-9-6
         (13) 978-0-9521413-9-6

© Peter Rothwell & Myrtle Ternstrom

Cover © Peter Rothwell

THE
LUNDY GRANITE COMPANY

An Industrial Adventure

Peter Rothwell
&
Myrtle Ternstrom

All rights reserved. No part of this publication may be reproduced, stored in a retrieval system, or transmitted in any form by any means electronic, mechanical, photocopying, scanning, recording or otherwise, without the prior written permission of the publishers.

Typeset, printed and bound by
Lazarus Press
Caddsdown Business Park
Bideford
Devon
EX39 3DX
WWW.LAZARUSPRESS.COM

'The Eastern Coast (from the Landing)'
Home Friend 1853

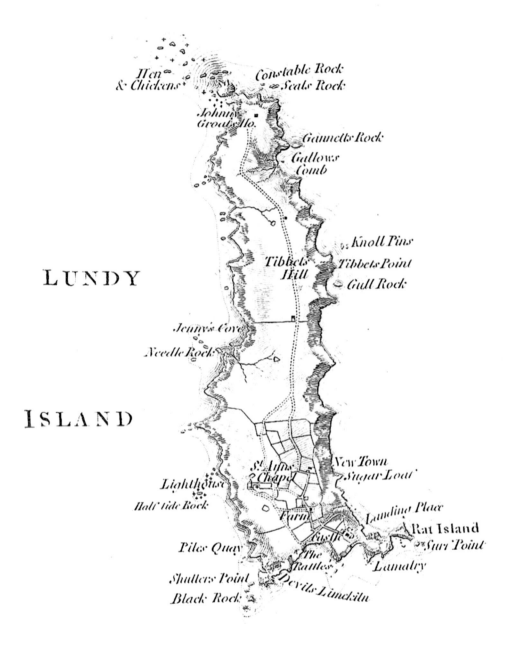

Reproduced from 1820 Ordnance Survey Map
Crown Copyright

CONTENTS

	page
INTRODUCTION	11
THE ISLAND & THE HEAVEN FAMILY	12
THE LUNDY GRANITE COMPANY	19
THE VILLAGE & THE QUARRY COMPLEX	29
QUARTER WALL COTTAGES	35
QUARRY COTTAGES	41
THE TIME-CHECK PLATFORM, UPPER PLATFORM & UPPER INCLINES	43
THE MAIN QUARRIES & MAIN PLATFORM	51
THE MAIN INCLINE	59
QUARRY QUAY	67
THE JETTY	74
THE END OF QUARRYING	83
HOPE REVIVED - A BUYER STEPS IN	93
THE JUDGEMENT OF THE COURT	100
THE CLOSING CHAPTER	103
AN AFTERWORD	108
APPENDICES	112
ACKNOWLEDGMENTS	177
REFERENCES & BIBLIOGRAPHY	178
INDEX	181

ILLUSTRATIONS

		page
	The Eastern Coast of Lundy	3
	1820 OS map of Lundy	4
1.	Bronze Age hut circle - Lundy, North End	11
2.	Members of the Heaven Family on the Landing Beach	12
3.	The Villa - Millcombe - c 1865	14
4.	William Hudson Heaven - c 1860	17
5.	The Heaven reserved area - 1863	18
6. & 7.	Cottages in the castle keep where WH Heaven housed his workers - c 1906	21
8.	Barton Cottages from St. Helen's Field (NB original pitched roofs) - c 1920	22
9.	The Tavern and Store interior - c 1900	22
10.	Lundy Granite Co. announcement of a second Share Issue. November 1863	24
11.	Share certificate issued by the Lundy Granite Co. in 1864	25
12.	Fremington Quay - circa 1945	25
13.	The Lighthouse and the Farm, Lundy - 1838	28
14.	The Village - circa 1872	28
15.	Plans showing construction work undertaken by LGC 1863 - 1868	30
16.	The Village from St. Helen's Church tower - circa 1960	30
17.	The Farmhouse with new south wing added by the Lundy Granite Co. c 1864	31
18.	Map showing main features of the quarry complex	32
19.	Aerial View of Quarry Cottages & Upper Complex	33
20.	Aerial view of Main Platform and Lower Inclines	33
21.	Quarter Wall Cottages - circa 1864	34
22.	Quarry Buildings adjacent to Quarter Wall	34
23.	Marks made by testing 'borers'	36
24. & 25.	Quarryman's tools	36
26. & 27.	Blocks of granite	37
28. & 29.	The remains of the Hospital - 1960s	38
30.	Date stone from Quarter Wall Cottages - 1864	39
31.	Interior of Quarry Cottages - 2008	39
32.	Quarry Cottages - 1927	40
33.	Quarry Cottages - 1960s	40
34.	The Upper Tramway - Timekeeper's Hut in the background	42
35.	The Timekeeper's hut - circa 1960	42
36.	The Time-check Platform & Timekeeper's Hut - 2008	44
37.	The Upper Platform & Cutting to Willlium Heard's Quarry - 2008	44
38.	The Upper Tramway from S East - 2008	45
39.	The Upper Platform, Time-check Platform & Timekeeper's Hut - 2008	45
40.	Court proceedings - the Times, 22 February 1868	47
41.	Unloading equipment on Landing Beach	48
42.	The Landing Beach slipway - c 1864	48
43.	Main Platform looking from the south - 1960s	49
44.	Sleeper marks on the Main Tramway looking south to Main Platform	49
45.	The Main Platform - c 1865 (artist's impression)	50
46.	The Main Platform - looking south - 2008	50
47.	The East Sidelands showing spoil tips associated with Smith's Pt. Quarry - 2008	52
48.	Looking south to Main Platform, the inclines & Quarry Cottages	53
49.	Remains of a small building, possibly a powder magazine	54
50.	Section of granite sleeper from Main Tramway	54

		page
51.	Main Tramway looking north showing sleeper marks - 2008	55
52. & 53.	A pair of trolley wheels found in the quarry area - c 1960	55
54.	The Quarry Complex as it might have appeard in 1865	56 & 57
55.	Possible brake drum arrangement	58
56.	Brake drum & 'Ratchet Steps'	58
57.	Masonry laid over the track-bed of Incline 1 to support track of Incline 2	60
58.	Site of 'Ratchet Steps'at the top of Main Incline - 2008	60
59. & 60.	Remains of brake drums at the top of Main Incline - 2008	61
61.	Vivian Quarry Incline -Llanberis, North Wales	62
62.	Remains of timber rail - Main Incline	64
63.	Timber rail and iron tie-bar - Main Incline	64
64.	Pair of timber rails	65
65.	Quarry Beach and Main Incline showing zig-zag inclined terraces	66
66.	Quarry Quay & Jetty - circa 1865	68
67.	Zig-zag inclined terraces at the base of the Main Incline	68
68.	Chanter's map 1877	69
69.	Detail from 1886 OS showing Quarry Beach & section of Main Incline	70
70.	Quarry Beach - outline of quay as observed in 2000	71
71.	Quarry Beach - outline of quay as observed in 2006	71
72.	Quay foundation blocks looking south	72
73.	Quay foundation blocks looking north	72
74. & 75.	Quay foundation blocks showing iron 'staples'	73
76.	Quarry Quay & Jetty as they might have appeared c 1867 (reconstruction)	74
77. & 78.	Jetty base blocks	76
79.	Map of Quarry Beach showing jetty base blocks and iron sockets	77
80.	Woody Bay Pier under construction - c 1897	77
81.	Cast-iron socket - sited on a rock in the middle of Quarry Beach	78
82.	Cast-iron socket - extreme SW corner of Quarry Beach	78
83.	Section of turned granite column	79
84.	Section of turned column showing worked triangular socket	79
85.	Section of finished granite sill & 'stapled' foundation blocks	80
86.	Section of wrought-iron rail	80
87.	A Heaven family outing on the Island - circa 1864	82
88.	William Hudson Heaven in 1869	92
89.	Old Broad Street London EC2 - location of National Bank & LGC office	95
90.	The Revd Hudson Grosett Heaven in 1869	96
91.	Frederick Wilkins 'Western Granite Co.' letterhead	104
92.	Smith's Point Quarry - posed photograph for LI&MQ prospectus - 1902	105
93.	Smith's Point Quarry - 2006	105
94.	Middle Quarry (VC Quarry) - 1949	107
95.	Sir Joseph Neale McKenna - circa 1867	110
96.	Lord Romilly, Master of the Rolls - 1851 - 1873	148

For all lovers of
LUNDY

Fig. 1 : *Bronze Age hut circle - Lundy, North End - (Peter Rothwell)*

INTRODUCTION

Lundy is a small island in the Bristol Channel where evidence survives that man has utilised the granite, of which Lundy is formed, for at least 10,000 years. The huts, walls and enclosures made by early man, using the unworked moorstone, can still be seen, most visibly at the north end of the island.

Since that time all construction work carried out on Lundy, with a few minor exceptions, has made use of the granite. Eventually, as the requirements of the builders and masons became more sophisticated, the crude moorstones were unsuitable and stone was extracted from small early quarries, some of which can still be identified.

It was not until the mid-nineteenth century, when the demand for robust stone for civil engineering projects and public works made the exportation of Lundy granite an increasingly viable proposition, that the final decision to quarry commercially was taken. William Hudson Heaven, the then owner, leased the island with quarrying rights to an enterprising entrepreneur and thus the way was clear for the Lundy Granite Company to be established.

What follows is an account of the events surrounding the short life and ignominious collapse of the Lundy Granite Company - it is the story of an industrial adventure, the effects of which are still evident to this day.

Fig. 2 : *Members of the Heaven Family on the Landing Beach (earliest known photograph showing the east sidelands without quarries) (Heaven archive)*

THE ISLAND AND THE HEAVEN FAMILY

The island of Lundy is a tableland orientated north-south at the mouth of the Bristol Channel, 11 miles north of the Devon coast at Hartland, with the nearest Devon ports at Ilfracombe, 23 miles to the east and Bideford 24.9 miles to the south east. The island is 3.1 miles in length north-south and approximately 0.5 miles wide at its broadest point, with an area of 1115 acres at sea level. The tidal range of 26ft is the second highest in the world.

There is only one landing place, which is at the south east of the island, with a fairly steep track to the summit. The landing bay, known as Lundy Roads, affords good anchorage with protection from the prevailing westerly winds. When the winds are north or easterly, ships cannot lie there and then landing is only possible by climbing from an access point at the base of the cliffs on the west coast.

Lundy's position presented a hazard to shipping, particularly when the 18th century expansion of trade led to a great increase in the volume and size of shipping in the Bristol Channel. This led to the construction of a tall lighthouse atop the island in 1820, which was augmented by a fog signal station low down on the west coast in 1862, and both were replaced in 1897 by the two low-level lighthouses at the north and south extremities.

Lundy is composed of a granite mass except at the south east corner, which consists of Upper Devonian metasedimentary rock, very similar to the Morte slates that form a contact junction with the granite in a line from the Sugar Loaf to the Rattles. The height of the plateau slopes gradually from 459 ft in the south to 295 ft in the north. The west coast is steep in character, where the rocks give magnificent scenery, while the east coast sidings are somewhat gentler and for the most part are green-blanketed.

The granite has been identified as belonging to the British Tertiary Volcanic Province, an igneous complex that includes the Isle of Skye and of which Lundy is the southernmost example, being around two million [hundred] years younger than the granite of Devon and Cornwall. Two principal types of granite were identified by Dollar (1941): the coarse-grained megacrystic granite, G1, and G2, a finer-grained megacrystic granite, both of which contain large white alkali feldspar crystals. Beryl, copper ore, feldspar, garnet, molybdenum, quartz and other minerals have been found (see Appendix XII). None of these occurs in commercially exploitable quantities.

Prior to 1969, when Lundy became the property of the National Trust, it had always been in private ownership or, in medieval times, appropriated by the Crown. The records for this go back to the twelfth century, when Henry II presented it to the Knights Templar. An interesting aspect of the island history is that although it was regarded as part of Devon, it has never been a parish in itself, nor formed part of one. Neither tithes nor taxes were levied, no controls were exercised nor services provided by mainland authorities, and its owners considered the island to be outside mainland jurisdiction. This rested on shaky justification, since it arose not from any charter or royally bestowed exemption, but from the prosaic fact that the island was hard to get to, so unimportant and so unlikely to return any profit that would exceed the cost of taxing it, that it was ignored. Before the quarries were set up the island was basically a farm: there was no church, no shop, and no school.

This was the state of the island when William Hudson Heaven (Fig. 4), a gentleman from Bristol, bought it in 1836 for £9,870. He was then 37 years of age, had been educated at Harrow and Oxford, completed the Grand Tour, and was married with a family of three sons and two daughters. At the age of 21 he had inherited sugar estates in Jamaica from his godfather, and he was said to have used the compensation money paid to plantation owners following the abolition of slavery (1834) for his purchase of Lundy. He intended it to be a summer resort for his family and friends, where the shooting could be enjoyed in season, and full advantage taken of the peace and beauty of the place itself.

Fig. 3 : *The Villa - Millcombe - circa 1865 - (Heaven archive)*

Heaven sought an assessment of the commercial viability of the granite. Thomas Spargo was commissioned to make a report and visited Lundy in 1839 and stated that he had found:

'…some excellent Granite Stone generally, but especially on the Eastern Side of the Island. I found very good stone for building Pier heads, Quays and Docks, and which might be brought to the place of shipping at a trifling expense and in consequence of such numerous quantity of Granite Stone on the Island, I think it would be advisable and advantageous to your Honor to cause a Place or kind of Quay to be erected for the purpose of vessels taking their cargoes.' - (Harman archive)

Despite Spargo's optimistic, but ill-informed, idea of a 'trifling expense' there could have been no question of Heaven's investing the sums that would be needed to set up the plant and to build a quay.

Heaven set about making the island suitable for a gentleman's summer residence: a modest villa was built in Millcombe (Fig. 3), the farmhouse was repaired and extended, and a trackway suitable for both carts and a carriage for the ladies was built from the landing place to the Villa that continued up to join the Trinity House track to the island plateau.

Heaven was forced to try to augment his finances. It occurred to him that the granite might be a saleable asset, and in 1838 he first of all offered to provide the granite for the building of the Royal Exchange in London free of charge. The reply he received was non-committal:

> My dear Sir,
> Immediately on receipt of your letter making an offer to the Committee for the Management of the Building of the Royal Exchange of sufficient granite from the island of Lundy, I caused the offer to be laid before the Committee. I have called at the Town Clerk's office to enquire what progress has been made. The reply was the gentleman had had several meetings on the subject of your liberal offer but as yet no decision had been come to - in a few days no doubt we shall get an answer. Please to present my kind regards to Mrs Heaven and believe me my dear Sir,
> Yours Truly,
> Tho. Helps   (Heaven archive)

This offer would presumably have involved the contractors taking out the granite themselves, which could have been of advantage to Heaven in the setting up of the necessary plant, and the advertisement for Lundy granite. If this was his idea, it was hardly a practical proposition for the builders concerned.

However, the expense of the works on Lundy was heavy and the earnings from the farm were negligible. In addition the income from the estates in Jamaica was in decline.. The abolition of slavery had been followed by the collapse of the market for cane sugar - partly because of the problems of labour and the disorder that followed the abolition, and partly because of competition from the rise of the sugar beet industry. Heaven also had the misfortune to lose money in a failed investment, so that with a growing family to provide for and educate, he could no longer carry the expense of an island that could not show a return on capital, but was a continuing drain on his pocket.

To ease the financial difficulties the island was leased to a tenant farmer in 1839, with just an area around Millcombe Valley and the southeast corner of the island reserved for the use of the Heaven family (Fig. 5). By this measure there was an income from the lease, and a reduction in the expenditure of running the farm while Heaven tried to sell the island. It was advertised in glowing terms in The Times in 1840:

> The mansion is of recent creation and embodies within it all the accommodation a patriotic little monarch can desire...the great source of revenue is yet to be divulged; First the extensive fishery...The granite throughout the island in the hands of an enterprising man will realise a fortune; the minerals including silver and copper have been discovered near the beach...The

sporting over the demesne is of the highest order and during the season myriads of little seabirds pay their annual visit and become tributary to the island by depositing countless of their eggs and dropping their beautiful feathers, all of which become a source of income....if specualtion is in view of the purchaser, there is such an abundance of stone as will enable him soon to erect a town upon this favoured isle, where the turmoil of politics will not disturb the harmony of the little monarch of the isle...happiness, contentment and independence will be as firmly fixed as the rock on which the island is placed. Communication from Bristol and Tenby is almost daily. *The Times*, 14 July 1840.

Two buyers responded, but neither of them took their offer forward to a purchase - possibly because it was found that the island did not correspond to the claims made for it. After these disappointments, Heaven took out mortgages against a family trust that by 1853 totalled a debt of £10,000 - more than he had paid for the island. In the meantime he continued with a lessee, but his finances were still a cause of acute anxiety.

The island was offered for sale again in 1856, but once more without success, so a surveyor was employed to report on the deposits of minerals and semi-precious stones. Although adits were opened to extract copper, the quantity obtained was not large and working them would have required an investment that was beyond Heaven's resources. But he was not ready to pass the possible advantages of these deposits to either a purchaser or a lessee. In 1858 he sought to secure Lundy as a government-funded Harbour of Refuge, with the additional advantage of the safe employment of convict labour on the island, but the proposal for Lundy was rejected as 'the depth of water in which the breakwater must be necessarily placed…is so great as…not to be thought of.'

The idea of the value of the granite was not forgotten, and Heaven submitted a sample of it to an International Exhibition in 1862 that received an honourable mention and a medal inscribed 'Class III'. This may have been the trigger that prompted a request in the following year from a William McKenna for a lease of the island to quarry the granite. The times were favourable to such an enterprise: there was a great need for robust building materials for the huge expansion in public works - the dockyards, bridges and roads that were needed to service a burgeoning industrial economy. A second impulse came from the Companies Act of 1862 that governed the formation of Joint Stock Companies so that the investors' liability was limited to the issued share capital.

Fig. 4 : *William Hudson Heaven - circa 1860 - (Heaven archive)*

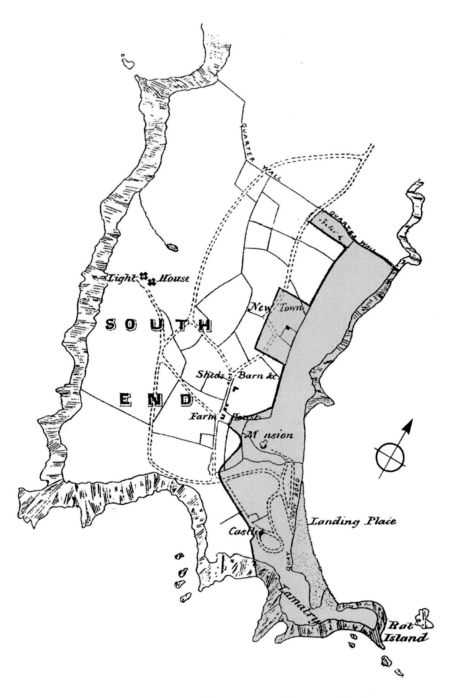

Fig. 5 : *The Heaven reserved area - 1863 - (Heaven archive)*

THE LUNDY GRANITE COMPANY

William McKenna did not intend to manage the quarries himself. Before he signed the lease he had made an agreement with the Lundy Granite Company Ltd that was to be launched by his brother, Joseph McKenna. The terms of the agreement were that the company would:

> ...purchase the lease, quarries, rights and interests of William Columban McKenna...in and about the island of Lundy...also to cultivate the island...the said W. C. McKenna agrees to sell and transfer all his right and interest in the said island and the granite thereon.

This agreement was signed on 10 July 1863, and the Lundy Granite Company Ltd was registered on 18 July. Heaven and, presumably, his solicitors were ignorant of the agreement, as a result no questions were raised about such a circuitous arrangement. In the light of subsequent events, the explanation for the arrangement lies in the benefits which were conferred on the lessee as given in the prospectus and the lease itself (Apppendix II). It is perhaps significant that the lessee, William McKenna, was not a shareholder in, nor a director of, the Lundy Granite Company.

The McKennas were an old-established Irish family: influential and well connected who held positions of power and influence. Joseph Neale and William Columban were sons of Michael McKenna who had married into the Irish aristocracy. Joseph McKenna, born in 1819, was called to the Irish Bar in 1849 and went on to become a JP, a knight in 1867 and was elected MP for Youghal in 1865 representing the Home Rule Party, and for South Monaghan in 1885 for the Irish Parliamentary Party.

He became chairman and managing director of the National Bank which had been founded as the National Bank of Ireland in 1835 by Daniel O'Connell (known as 'The Liberator', O'Connell was Ireland's predominant political leader in the first half of the nineteenth century). Joseph McKenna saw the bank prosper through the 1850s and 60s but he, along with other directors, was finally removed from the board in 1869 as a result of having involved the bank with some questionable and highly speculative accounts.

William Columban McKenna, two years younger than his brother Joseph, was a different kind of character. He was born on board ship en route for America (both his father and grandfather lived for some time in Philadelphia). He was advised by Daniel O'Connell to return to England where, through O'Connell's patronage, he was appointed Surveyor of Taxes by the Board of Stamps and Taxes. ...'a position which was ill suited to M'Kenna's impulsive and restless character and his inherent antagonism to authority.' (Appendix XIII). In 1859, William McKenna was Surveyor of Taxes investigating the affairs of The South Yorkshire Railway Company and he proved to be a highly astute official. Three years later he negotiated the lease with William Hudson Heaven.

William McKenna fathered seven children, the youngest of whom, Reginald, had an illustrious political career as President of the Board of Education and First Lord of the Admiralty; eventually achieving high ministerial office as Chancellor of the Exchequer to the Asquith government of 1915. He resigned when Lloyd George became Prime Minister, ended his career as director of the Midland Bank with a Knighthood.

By aggreement work was put in hand even before the lease was signed in August of 1863. A tenure of 14 years was granted, with the option to terminate after 7 years provided that one year's notice was given, or to renew for a further 14 years. It gave possession of the whole island, including the farm, but with the exception of a designated area in the southeast of the island that was reserved for the Heavens. For them it would mean that some sacrifice of the island peace was inevitable, but the Villa in Millcombe Valley was well sheltered, the reserved area was entirely private, and the relief from financial anxiety was a blessing. The lease is a lengthy document with many detailed conditions and stipulations laid upon the lessee, even down to the handling of manure, which could have caused friction between lessee and landlord had either party paid due attention to them (Appendix II).

With this lease the future seemed to be set fair for Heaven's getting a considerable income, with a reduction in his expenses, and without the need for any capital investment. Best of all, perhaps, was that he would not have to leave his island home. In 1851, as part of the necessary economies, the family had made Lundy their permanent home and they were undoubtedly very attached to it. In 1863 the population consisted of two families at the Lighthouse, two more at the Fog Signal Station, the Heaven family and their servants at the Villa, the labourers housed in the cottages within the castle (Figs. 6 & 7), and the bailiff and his family at the farmhouse. Things were about to change.

Excursion to Lundy Island

'...the steam boat *Henry Southan* left Instow pier at half past six a.m. with about 150 excursionists, for Lundy Island. The weather was delightful, a strong breeze blowing from the westward, and the passage, which occupied two and half hours, was much enjoyed... On arriving, anchor was dropped in Lundy Roads, landing being effected by boats... The table land is about 2,000 acres in extent, the greater part of which is under cultivation, the rest being covered with fern, heath and furze, which affords excellent fodder for the store cattle... Ere another season rolls round...it is fair to suppose that the new beautiful sections of granite which adorn the cliffs – the wild rose heather of the sidings and English gorse on the table land – will have been experimented on by the plough-share and miners hammer of the new London granite company who have recently rented that Island of the proprietor... for the purpose of working the granite quarries and improving the soil for the production of food for the miners and increased population. The Buckland wood houses have already been purchased by Mr Smith, of Emmetts Grange, and will be transported to their new site in the course of a week or two. In the interim, preparatory steps are being taken for launching the whole scheme...' (The Bideford Gazette - 23rd August 1863)

Figs. 6 (looking NW) & 7 (looking SE):
*Cottages in the castle keep where W. H. Heaven housed his workers - circa 1894 -
(Heaven archive)*

Fig. 8 : *Barton Cottages from St. Helen's Field showing original pitched roofs - circa 1920 (Alfred Blackwell)*

Fig. 9 : *The Tavern & Stores, interior - circa 1900 - (Ternstrom collection)*

> **Excerpts from the Prospectus of the Lundy Granite Company Ltd, 1863**
>
> 'The specimens of Granite from the Island shewn at the International Exhibition of 1862, received from the commissioners an 'HONOURABLE MENTION OF THE FIRST CLASS', and the colour and texture were much admired by some of the best judges of the stone'
>
> '. . .it is estimated that the cost of producing the stone will be less than that of any other Granite quarry in the kingdom.'
>
> 'The farm. . . covers an area of about 1,400 acres. It is capable of producing considerable profit under judicious management. . . and the supply of the produce to the workmen at a moderate cost.'
>
> '. . .the island of Lundy which I have visited, would be the cheapest place in England to open Granite Quarries, because the Granite is on the surface; there is no head of any consequence to be taken away, and the place is well adapted for a ship to load as there is a natural-formed Harbour, where ships could load without difficulty. . . others have a great deal of land carriage before getting to a port or rail.'

The company was to raise a capital of £25,000 in £5 shares, with the directors permitted to borrow up to one half of the value of the paid-up shares provided that they obtained the approval of the shareholders at an extraordinary general meeting. Heaven was to receive a yearly rent of £500, plus basic royalties of £200 and an additional percentage based on the weight of the granite exported.

A notice in The Times of 28 October 1863 drew attention to the prospectus for the Lundy Granite Co., (Appendix VIII) with the information that 'The company have a contract to supply the stone for the first section of the Thames Embankment.'

On the strength of a stated contract to supply granite for the Thames Embankment to be built in London, and that the value of the granite required for this would be £100,000, the share capital of the company was raised by that amount in November 1863 by an issue of 20,000 shares at £5 each. It was implied that the contract was under way and that it was necessary to raise the capital accordingly, but the truth of the matter was that the company had got no further than submitting samples of the granite to the contractors.

An advertisement in the same paper on 3 November 1863 (Fig. 10) announced an extension of the capital from £25,000 to £100,000 in a further issue of £5 shares. It is stated that the first issue was fully subscribed, which appears not to have been true, that the specimen of Lundy granite sent (by Mr Heaven) to the International Exhibition in 1862 obtained 'Honourable Mention of the First Class,' whereas the medal awarded to Mr Heaven is inscribed 'Class III', and that the Company had secured the contract for the supply of granite for the Thames Embankment, which it had not.

Bilston, 3d November, 1863.

THE LUNDY GRANITE COMPANY (Limited). Extension of capital from £25,000 to £100,000, in £5 shares. Deposit 10s. per share on application, and £1 on allotment.

DIRECTORS.

Harvey Lewis, Esq., M.P., Director of the National Bank, Grosvenor-street, W.
F. B. Henshaw, Esq., Director of the National Bank, Finchley New-road
Hon. R. Howe Browne, Chertsey
P. G. Vanderbyl, Esq., Upper Hyde-park-gardens
J. N. McKenna, Esq., Director of the National Bank, Inverness-terrace, W.

Bankers—The National Bank, 13, Old Broad-street, London, with its branches; and the National Bank of Liverpool (Limited).
Brokers—Messrs. Hichens, Harrison, and Co., 21, Threadneedle-street; Edward Fox, Esq., Dublin

Offices: 17, Old Broad-street, London.

This Company has been formed for some months with a capital of £25,000, fully subscribed.

The immense mass of granite, of superior quality, at Lundy Island, the specimens of which obtained Honourable Mention of the First Class at the International Exhibition of 1862, has secured for the existing Company a contract for the supply of granite for the first section of the Thames Embankment, which alone amounts to about £100,000 worth of stone. The Company find the demand for their granite to be practically unlimited, and, as they enjoy singular advantages for the cheap production of the highest quality of stone, they have resolved on the increase of the capital from 5,000 shares of £5 each to 20,000 shares of £5 each; the public are, therefore, offered a participation in the enterprise on equal terms with the present shareholders.

There are no free shares, and no promotion fees.

The Island has been taken in perpetuity from the lessee on the terms that he is to have one-half the profits over £10 per cent. per annum.

Detailed prospectuses can be had at the bankers, brokers, and offices of the Company.

Fig. 10: *Lundy Granite Co announcement of a second Share Issue.*
The Times, November 1863

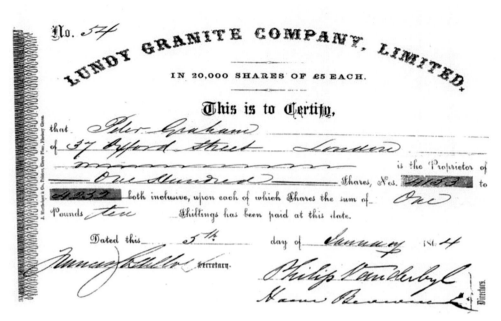

Fig. 11: *Share certificate issued by the Lundy Granite Co. in 1864 - (Tom Baker)*

Fig. 12: *Fremington Quay circa 1945 - (Rothwell collection)*

By July 1864 15,480 shares had been taken up, with an initial payment of £1.10s per share, giving a working capital of £23,220. The value of each share was £5, and after the initial payment, the directors of the company could, and did, demand further payments from the shareholders as the need arose. They were able to make calls only to the maximum value of each share of £5, but if the shareholder did not pay the call, his share would be forfeited.

At the time of this advertisement the contract had not been secured. An investigation was carried out by The Metropolitan Board of Works in 1868 into the awarding of the contract, to hear the cases of two MPs who had been involved, one of whom was a member of the Board of Works. He had influenced the awarding of the contract after he had secured the agreement of the prospective contractor or negotiator (a Mr Furness) that only granite from the Lundy Granite Co. would be used. There had been an attempt by Furness to cover this by ascribing this negotiation to the other MP who was involved (and who was also representing another interest in the Lundy Granite Company). There had been dishonest dealings, and the MP concerned had to resign from the Metropolitan Board (Fig. 40).

Not only did the Lundy Granite Co. not have the contract, but it was in fact a sub-contractor to the Dartmoor Granite Company that was not awarded the contract to supply Mr Furness until 22 November 1865, on which date the contract with the Lundy Granite Co. was also signed. It would appear that on the strength of the dubious arrangements made between the parties in 1863, the Lundy Granite Co. had claimed to have secured the contract in order to increase their capital, and had gone ahead with the establishment of the granite works straight away.

One factor not generally noticed at the time, but that would later prove to be significant, was that most of the directors of the company (including Joseph McKenna, brother of the lessee) were also directors of the National Bank that handled the company's finances. The two companies used the same solicitors, the same brokers, and had adjacent premises in London that were shared with other concerns in which the bank and the company had a common interest.

A vessel was needed to service the establishment of the works on Lundy and, eventually to transport the granite, and the *Vanderbyl*, chosen by and named after one of the Lundy Granite Company directors, was acquired for £3000. Two depots were established on the mainland to connect with railway services: one at Fremington (Fig. 12) about 20 miles away on the mainland and one at Highbridge in Somerset. The Fremington depot was managed by Edward McKenna, possibly a relative of William and Joseph.

'MODERN ROBINSON CRUSOE'
FORTY-THREE YEARS' EXPERIENCES ON LUNDY ISLAND, MR. HEAVEN TELLS A STIRRING STORY.
HAS BEEN THE CLERGYMAN, SCHOOLMASTER, AND FRIEND OF HIS PEOPLE; AN ISLAND WITHOUT RATES, TAXES, POVERTY, OR IDLENESS

LUNDY QUARRIES

'How long did your father live on the island?'

'He bought it in 1836, and died here in 1883. He was 84 years of age. The inhabitants of the island at the present time number between 30 and 40; in my father's time, when the granite quarries were being worked here, there were 400 people on the island.'

'Will you tell me something about those quarries?'

'Yes. A company approached my father and got a lease for twenty-one years, renewable in perpetuity, subject to periodical revaluation to decide whether rents should be raised or reduced. But it was an unbusinesslike company. Before they had built a cottage on the island they engaged fifty stone-cutters from Scotland on a three years' agreement at 5s a day and sent them here. The first thing they asked for was housing accommodation, and they were told they must build cottages. They were simply stone-cutters, and did not know how to build. This is an instance in which the whole thing was carried through, the money being thrown into the sea.

'They had a capital of £100,000, which was a big amount in those days, and they spent £80,000 of it. Forty thousand pounds went in directors' fees and that sort of thing. The quarry was worked for six years, and a good deal of the stone was exported. The company took a large contract for supplying granite for the Thames Embankment, and sent up a specially-picked stone as a sample. This was accepted, and some of the stones from this island are in the foundations of Westminster Bridge to-day. They were pressed to supply stone according to sample, but they sent inferior stone, and the contract was cancelled. The stone, as a result got into bad odour in the market. All the experts said that those quarries should have undersold any other quarry in England, because there was no land carriage. You had simply to let the stone down by its own weight from the cliff into the ship. Well, the workmen who lived here at that time lived in temporary accommodation made of corrugated iron and wood, and when the company came to grief they were taken away and sold. The cottages fell to ruin, because it would not have paid my father to keep them in repair when there was no one to live in them.'

'Western Mail' - August 9th 1906.

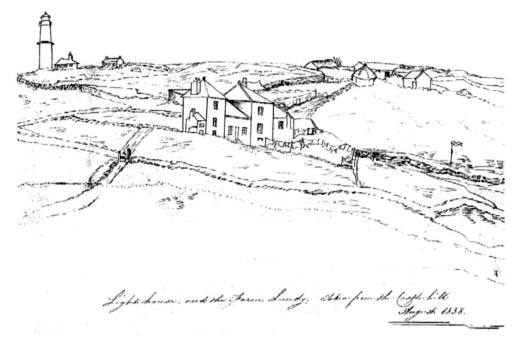

Fig. 13: *The Lighthouse & Farm - circa 1838 - (Heaven archive)*

Fig. 14: *The Village - circa 1872 - (Heaven archive)*

THE VILLAGE & THE QUARRY COMPLEX

The precise extent of the company's building work at the farm, on the enclosing walls and in what is now known as the Village, is not absolutely certain, but the shippons (cattle sheds), a barn, and the pigs' enclosure pre-date the quarry company's building work (Fig. 15). The company built a row of eight labourers' cottages, then called Sea View (Fig. 8), in what is now called the High Street and to the south of them an iron hut was erected, which served as the school, for church services, and as a general meeting room. A fine self-contained south wing, intended for the eventual manager, was added to the farmhouse (Fig. 17), but was left unfinished internally. There had never been a shop on Lundy, and socialising between the few inhabitants had always taken place in the kitchen of the farmhouse until the company built a canteen and store (Fig. 9). The store formed part of another self-contained wing on the north side of the farmhouse. It also housed a bakery, a separate cottage for the store-keeper, and a range of out-buildings.

In order to house the quarrymen and builders, wooden barracks were put up and enclosed by stone walls in the areas known latterly as the Fowl Run and the Rick Yard (Fig. 15). They were roofed with felt and covered with black tar, were not beautiful, and were christened ironically as 'Golden Square' by the Heaven family. The officers of the company took over the farmhouse, and an extensive building programme was undertaken both for the establishment of the works and the provision of dwellings and facilities for the Company officers and the labour force. In due time a prefabricated iron Mission Hut was put up where the sheep dip now is, that was used as a meeting room, a school, and for services.

As the farm buildings and stables were taken over by the company, the Heaven family had to provide replacements for these for their own use within the reserved area. Stables were built by the gates up to the Villa, and at the east end of the gardens, with a cow house nearby. Small walled gardens were cultivated along the east sidings, and shooting paths cleared as far as Quarter Wall. The whole of the reserved private area was fenced, and the Castle Field and Castle Hill field were kept for the family's own arable use.

The quarry works and the quarries themselves were cut into the sheltered eastern sidelands, some way to the north of the Landing Bay. A wide terrace, the Main Platform, (Figs. 43 - 46), sited approximately halfway up the sideland, was levelled as a marshalling area where the rough granite blocks were unloaded from the trolleys used to transport them down the tramway from the quarries. On the western side of the Main Platform, sheds, or 'bankers', with open fronts to allow the dust to be carried away, were built into the sideland to provide shelter for the stonemasons while they worked the granite. At the southern end of the Main Platform, a steep incline was cut into the sideland to carry the stone down to sea level, and to bring up goods and supplies. Access to the quarries from the island plateau was by a steep path down the sideland to the north end of the Main Platform. Before the quarrymen descended the path to go to work

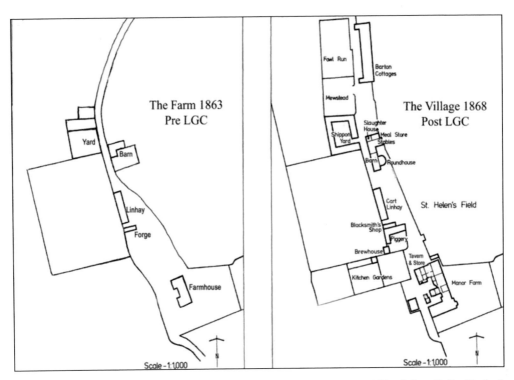

Fig. 15: *Comparative plans of the Village pre & post LGC 1863 - 1868 - (after Colin Taylor)*

Fig. 16: *The Village from St. Helen's Church tower - circa 1960 - (Derek Sach)*

they would have clocked in at the time-keeper's hut on the Time-check Platform (Fig. 36) where a clock-face was displayed in the round aperture that now accommodates a memorial tablet to Felix Gade, Mr. Harman's agent on the island. Below the Main Platform, a walled path was made down to the level of a stone-built quay and a wooden jetty on Quarry Beach.

A tramway with a southern gradient was laid leading north from the Main Platform for the trucks or trolleys that carried the stone from the quarries. It is likely that horses were used to haul the trolleys to and from the quarries - three granite quarries were operational although others had been opened up for trials. Immediately below the Time-check Platform was the Upper Platform where the stone from the first quarry, William Heard's Quarry, (Figs. 18 & 19) was prepared either for the construction work taking place on the island or for transportation to the mainland. The remains of an open-fronted granite structure, probably a 'banker' can also be seen on this platform. The steep path leading down from the Time-check Platform to the main working area and the path down to Quarry Beach from the Main Platform are still in use today.

Fig. 17: *The Farmhouse with the new south wing added circa 1864 by the Lundy Garanite Co.*
(Heaven archive)

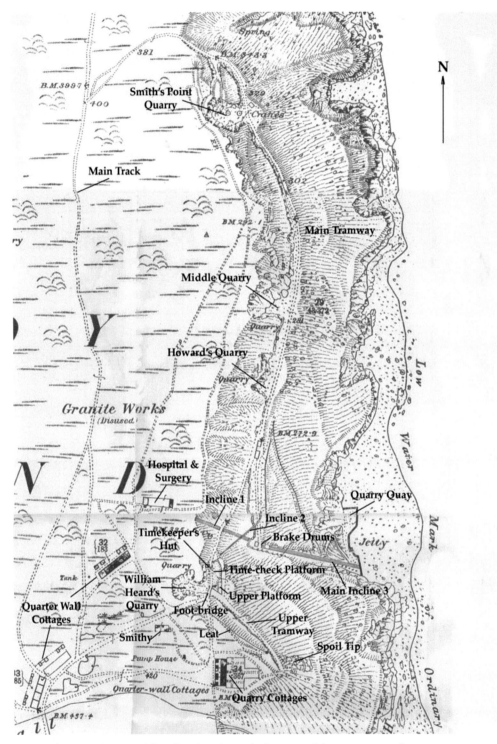

Fig. 18: *Map showing the main features of the quarry complex (reproduced from the 1886 OS map - Crown Copyright)*

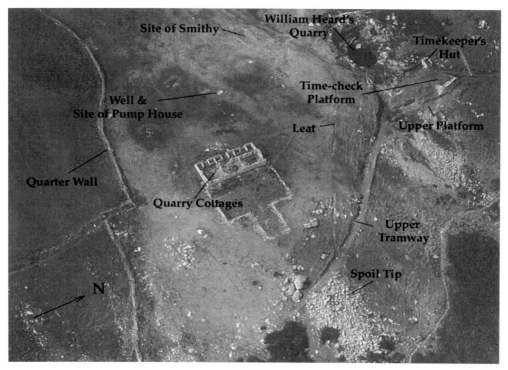

Fig. 19: *Aerial view of Quarry Cottages and Upper Complex - (NMR 1996)*

Fig. 20: *Aerial view of the Main Platform and lower inclines - (NMR 1996)*

Fig. 21 : *Quarter Wall Cottages - circa 1864 (reconstruction - Peter Rothwell)*

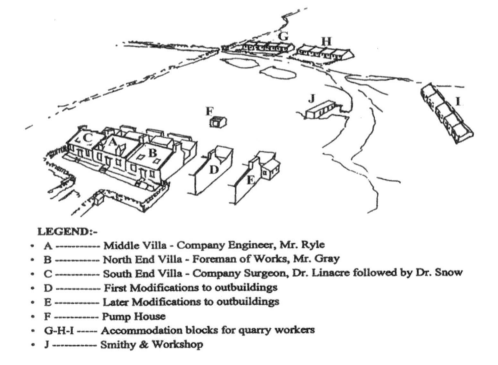

LEGEND:-
- A ------------ Middle Villa - Company Engineer, Mr. Ryle
- B ------------ North End Villa - Foreman of Works, Mr. Gray
- C ------------ South End Villa - Company Surgeon, Dr. Linacre followed by Dr. Snow
- D ------------ First Modifications to outbuildings
- E ------------ Later Modifications to outbuildings
- F ------------ Pump House
- G-H-I ----- Accommodation blocks for quarry workers
- J ------------ Smithy & Workshop

Fig. 22 : *Quarry Buildings adjacent to Quarter Wall (Peter Rothwell)*

QUARTER WALL COTTAGES

The island plateau is an undulating moor partitioned by three walls that run across the Island; Quarter Wall, Halfway Wall and Threequarter Wall. Immediately north of Quarter Wall, adjacent to the track leading to the north of the island, the company constructed three blocks of cottages for the quarrymen (Fig. 21), a small hospital, a surgery, and a row of three splendidly-sited cottages for the quarry officers. The ruins of these cottages and the hospital remain, as do the foundations of three rows of workers' cottages, with associated wells. Evidence of a smithy or forge, is also apparent. Building work evidently continued throughout the working period of the quarries, as one row of cottages and another building were still incomplete when the company ceased operation. But in 1864 with some of these buildings already completed and in use; an engineer, a manager, a doctor, an accountant appointed; a work force of more than two hundred men, including the *Vanderbyl* and her crew, in place, quarrying could begin in earnest.

Of the three accommodation blocks planned for the employees just to the north of Quarter Wall (Fig. 22) only two of the Blocks, G and H (referred to as Quarter Wall Cottages, Fig. 21), were fully completed.

It is interesting to compare the ground plan and dimensions of what little remains of Quarter Wall Cottages with those of Quarry Cottages and Barton Cottages. Estimated measurements suggest that they were similar in layout and included outbuildings to the rear or to the side of each block. This theory provides the justification for the visual reconstruction of the buildings (Fig. 21). It would have made sense, if the stone masons had to produce a considerable number of door and window frames and lintels, that they did so to a pattern. There are two wells associated with Quarter Wall Cottages, one situated behind accommodation block G and the other beside the main track to the west of accommodation block 'I' (see Fig. 22).

The building that stands to the north east of Quarter Wall Cottages is all that remains above ground level of the Company's hospital (Figs. 28 & 29) which consisted of two similar buildings, possibly a surgery and a ward or clinic, connected by a low wall enclosing an open area, possibly a garden.

To the north-west of Quarry Cottages it is possible to make out a small platform cut into the bank to the south of the track between Quarter Wall Cottages and Quarry Cottages; (Langham, 1994, 172) identifies this as the 'Pump House'. A good deal of slag, clinker, cinder and coal waste has been found at this site which indicates that the site was a smithy, forge and repair shop for the equipment and machinery of the original quarry (William Heard's Quarry - Figs. 18 & 19). The Pump House (shown as 'F' in Fig. 22) in fact refers to the covered pump at the well-head which served Quarry Cottages; the exposed upper walls of which are still evident.

Just to the east of Quarry Cottages can be seen a granite lined leat or drain that would have diverted surface water away from the workings now known as

Quarry Pond. On the high ground between the site of the Smithy, the well-head (Pump House) and Quarry Cottages, it is still possible to see where the quarrymen tested the hand-borers and 'swell jumpers' that were used to drill the granite prior to splitting (Fig. 23). Worn out and discarded tools have also been found at this location.

Fig. 23 :
Marks made by testing 'borers'after 're-tipping''by the black-smith (Peter Rothwell)

Figs. 24 & 25
Quarrymen's tools
(Rothwell collection)

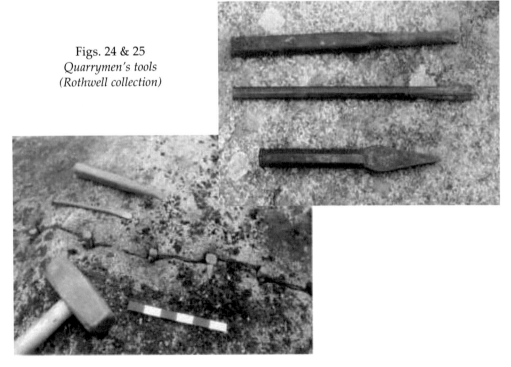

Figs. 26 :& 27
Blocks of granite that remain in the quarry complex, showing marks left by drills &'borers', 'plugs' & 'feathers'
(Peter Rothwell)

Fig. 27 :

Fig. 28 : *The remains of the Hospital from SE - 1960s - (Derek Sach)*

Fig. 29 : *The remains of the Hospital from SW - 1960s - (Derek Sach)*

Fig. 30 : *Date stone found adjacent to site of Quarter Wall Cottages - (Peter Rothwell)*

Fig. 31 : *The interior of Quarry Cottages - 2008 - (Peter Rothwell)*

Fig. 32 : *Quarry Cottages - 1927 - (Ternstrom collection)*

Fig. 33 : *The remains of Quarry Cottages - 1960s - (Derek Sach)*

QUARRY COTTAGES

The Quarry Managers' cottages are shown on the 1886 OS map as 'Quarter Wall Cottages' (Fig. 18) but they were referred to by the Lundy Granite Co. as South End Villa, Middle Villa and North End Villa. The Heaven family later called them the South, Mid and North Cottages, and then 'Belle View'. and in the National Trust Archaeological Survey they are referred to as 'Old Quarry Cottages'. The three accommodation blocks were known to the Heavens as Quarter Wall Cottages. We shall adopt this nomenclature and refer to the managers' cottages as Quarry Cottages.

There is clear structural evidence that Quarry Cottages underwent a series of alterations during their useful life, particularly to the rear outbuildings. Various modifications were made to improve conditions and amenities. Windbreaks were added and there is also evidence of alterations to reduce the width of the rear access ways to provide some relief from the westerly winds. (Fig. 22).

The original sanitary arrangements are unlikely to have been any more sophisticated than earth closets with nothing but the crudest of drainage or disposal systems. However, there is evidence of what appear to be several attempts to improve this facility. It is clear from the traces of mortar and cement left on the exterior north and south facing walls that various lean-to structures have been built against them. Large square terracotta tiles and the remains of a salt-glazed soil pipe are still visible close to the north wall indicating that this was probably the site of a relatively sophisticated WC (Fig. 22). As South End Villa was in use as late as 1921, it is not unreasonable to assume that these improvements commenced when the Heaven family prepared the properties for renting around 1872.

To the rear of the southernmost cottage, between it and its attendant outbuildings, are the remains of what could be a granite stand and a brick hearth for a copper, which would have been used to provide hot water for laundry. It appears that water was supplied through a down pipe that would probably have fed rain water into a butt.

To the east frontage of Quarry Cottages a flower-bed approx. 1m wide and retained by granite curbs ran the length of the building immediately beneath the windows; Narcissi still blossom here each spring. The bed was divided by granite steps that led from each front door to a path that connected the three cottages (Fig. 19). From this path a further short flights of steps led down a sloping bank to the main garden, the boundary walls of which still extend for 45m toward the east sideland.

The lintel, portico and supporting corbels that grace the east door of Government House were taken from the main door of the quarry manager's cottage, (the central one of the three). As the cottages were the residences for the senior company officials, and then the Heaven family guests, it is likely that the pump over the well would have been covered if not completely enclosed; hence the term Pump House.

Fig. 34 : *The Upper Tramway showing the marks where stone 'sleepers' would have been. The Timekeeper's hut in the background - circa 1960 - (Derek Sach)*

Fig. 35 : *The Timekeeper's hut - circa 1960 - (Derek Sach)*

THE TIME-CHECK PLATFORM, UPPER PLATFORM AND UPPER INCLINES

Today the path that leads from Quarry Cottages to the Time-check platform descends into a cutting that terminates in Quarry Pond. This is the site of the earliest Lundy Granite Company (LGC) working and is identified as William Heard's Quarry (Figs. 18 & 19). The tramway (Fig. 34) leading from the quarry to the Upper Platform and the spoil tips on the upper east sidelands passed through the cutting which was spanned by a wooden foot-bridge linking the Time-check Platform to the path from Quarry Cottages. The original timekeeper's hut (Figs. 34 & 35), now restored as a memorial to Felix Gade (agent for the Harmans between 1926 and 1969) and known universally as 'Gi's Hut', stands on the Time-check Platform. A commemorative plaque now occupies the circular recess that once accommodated the time-clock. As previously mentioned, immediately below and to the east of this is the Upper Platform from which a tramway extends southward to a series of spoil tips (Fig. 18).

On the Upper Platform can be seen the remains of what appear to have been lean-to buildings. Here the granite from William Heard's Quarry, would have been worked and dressed before being transported to wherever it was required on the Island or lowered to the Main Platform down a single-track incline, (Incline 2, Fig. 18). William Heard's Quarry would most probably have provided material for much of the initial construction work undertaken by the LGC on the island .

On the east sidelands to the east of the Hospital, evidence remains of the three inclines associated with the quarry workings. Incline 1 ran from the edge of the plateau, just east of the Hospital, to the Main Platform and is shown on the 1886 OS as a twin-track incline. Incline 2, a single-track incline, ran from the Upper Platform to the Main Platform, whilst Incline 3, which had twin tracks, ran from the southern end of the Main Platform down to the Quay and the jetty (Fig. 18).

The mechanics of the upper inclines are still not fully understood, neither is the sequence in which the quarries were opened. What is clear is that a reliable source of stone was needed for the immense amount of construction work involved in creating the infrastructure for a commercial quarrying operation. It is fair to assume that William Heard's Quarry was used to provide granite for construction work on the island. For commercial exploitation the sources would need to be much more impressive and more easily accessible. These sources were opened up as the Main Platform took shape and the main tramway was extended northward. The establishment and development of the necessary infrastructure for a commercial enterprise would also have demanded the importation of immense amounts of material. Therefore some method of moving the worked granite, materials, supplies and equipment up and down the steep sidelands would have been used prior to the commissioning of the Main Incline (Incline 3) from the Main Platform to the new quay and jetty. It was for this purpose that the first two of the three inclines and the main tramway would have been constructed.

Fig. 36 : *The Time-check Paltform & Timekeeper's hut ('Gi;s Hut') from East - 2008*
(Peter Rothwell)

Fig. 37 : *The Upper Platform and cutting to William Heard's Quarry from East - 2008*
(Peter Rothwell)

Fig. 38 : *The Upper Tramway looking S East- 2008 -(Peter Rothwell)*

Fig. 39 : *The Upper Platform, Time-check Platform & Timekeeper's hut from East - 2008 (Peter Rothwell)*

The line of the cutting for the earliest incline (Incline 1) can still be seen, running from the plateau immediately east of the hospital to the southern end of the Main Platform adjacent to the brake drums that controlled the Main Incline (Incline 3). Until recently it was thought that Incline 2 had been the first to be constructed (Langham, 1994), but investigations have revealed that masonry constructed as a support for the incline (Incline 2) from the Upper Platform, had been laid over the track of Incline 1 (Langham, 1994, 177) states that this incline (Incline 1) from the Upper Platform to the Main Platform was controlled by a brake drum using a loaded tub or sled as a counter-weight. However, this would not have been possible if the accuracy of the surveyors and cartographers for the 1886 OS map is to be relied upon as the incline is shown there as a single-track incline . This contention is born out by the relative widths of what remains of the cuttings

It might be useful at this juncture to consider some of the factors confronting the Lundy Granite Company when it came to selecting the best site for the quay and jetty and the main incline. It is clear that from the earliest days of the enterprise the LGC would have needed some facility for landing materials and supplies on the island. Within the terms of the lease, the LGC had access to the Landing Beach but it had also undertaken to repair and maintain the roads and tracks it used, and this would have been a considerable drain on its resources. This factor and the tremendous problems involved in transporting the granite and other goods between the quarries and the Landing Beach, coupled with the immense difficulties of loading and unloading vessels from the beach without a proper jetty (Figs. 41 & 42), would have compelled the Company to make the construction of its own purpose-built quay and jetty its first priority.

The lease allowed the Company the option of siting the quay and jetty at Gannet's Bay, a mile or so north of the quarries. This would have provided a relatively sheltered landing and deeper water, but for ease of access a site directly below the workings, now known as Quarry Beach, was chosen. The fact that this jetty was only accessible at high water and when the wind was westerly would have had a bearing on the viability of the enterprise; it would have been impossible to guarantee regular shipments .

Conjecture about how the inclines worked begins at the head of Incline 1 on the edge of the sideland east of the Hospital. This incline is shown as a twin-track incline on the 1886 OS and was the first of the three inclines to be constructed. There is no evidence remaining of this incline other than that which is indicated on the OS map and the depression in the sideland left by the cutting. The fact that a short length of retaining wall, which would have supported the track of Incline 2, still exists and is laid on the bed of Incline 1, confirms the sequence for the construction of these two inclines. It is not clear how the tubs were controlled on Incline 1 but it was most likely that a similar arrangement to that which was subsequently used on the Main Incline (Incline 3), was employed, namely counter-weight. It is perfectly possible that the brake drums, cables, and even the tubs and tracks that were first employed on Incline 1 and 2 were transferred lock, stock and barrel to the Main Incline.

Langham suggests (1994, 179) that the controlling mechanism for Incline 2 was a vertical brake wheel or winding wheel rigged on a gantry mounted adjacent to the Upper Platform. There is no evidence remaining of the massive structure that would have been needed to support this system, nor is the masonry of the platform itself sufficiently well bonded to have been able to withstand the stresses that such a system would have imposed upon it.

It is more likely that a fairly crude system of cables anchored at the top of the sideland above the platform would have been employed for lowering and lifting the loaded tubs or sleds. It is also possible that the machinery used to drive or control this incline was not sited on the Upper Platform, but at the base of the incline on the Main Platform. If this were the case it would obviate the need for heavy equipment on the Upper Platform and would explain the single track configuration of Incline 2, since the only mechanism required at the head of the incline would have been a well anchored pulley wheel or block around which the chain or cable attached to the tub would run.

> M'CLEAN V. THE LUNDY GRANITE COMPANY (LIMITED).
>
> Mr. Pollock, Q.C., Mr. J. C. Mathew, and Mr. A. Wilson appeared for the plaintiffs; Mr. Prentice, Q.C., and Mr. Murphy for the defendants.
>
> The plaintiffs in this case were Messrs. M'Clean, Stillman, and Bovill, trading as the Dartmoor Granite Company, and the defendants were the Lundy Granite Company. At the close of last year the plaintiffs had a contract to supply granite to Mr. Furness for the Thames Embankment, and in order to supply it they entered into a contract on the 22d of November with defendants for the purchase of 24,000 cubic feet of their Lundy Island granite. This amount was to be delivered at the rate of 1,000ft. a week, to commence a month after the order. The granite was to be equal to the Dartmoor granite supplied by the plaintiffs, and to be subject to the approval of the engineer on the works. Between 3,000ft. and 4,000ft. were delivered under the contract, and this was admitted by the defendants to have been in bad condition, so as to require re-dressing; and in respect of this money was paid into court. According to the plaintiffs' witnesses the granite was also very inferior in quality to the Dartmoor granite, and was rejected by Mr. Furness's engineer and by the officer of the Board of Works on this ground. Finally, on the 12th of June last, the plaintiffs wrote, giving this reason, and telling the defendants not to send any more of their granite. The case ultimately resolved itself into a question whether this letter amounted to a rescission of the contract.
>
> At the close of Mr. Prentice's opening for the defence, on the suggestion of his Lordship, it was agreed to take a nominal verdict for the plaintiffs, and refer the matter to the Court.

Fig. 40 : *Court proceedings - The Times, 22 February 1868*

Fig. 41 : *Unloading equipment on Landing Beach - (Ternstrom collection)*

Fig. 42 : *The Landing Beach slipway - circa 1864 (H G Heaven 3rd from left)*
(Heaven archive)

Fig. 43 : *The Main Platform from the south - 1960s - (Derek Sach)*

Fig. 44 : *Sleeper marks on Main Tramway looking south to Main Platform - 2008 (Peter Rothwell)*

Fig. 45 : *The Main Platform - circa 1865 - (artist's impression, Peter Rothwell)*

Fig. 46: *The Main Platform, - looking south - 2008 - (Peter Rothwell)*

THE MAIN QUARRIES AND MAIN PLATFORM

There is little evidence to indicate in which particular sequence the quarries were opened up once the construction of the tramway from the Main Platform northward had commenced. However, it is reasonable to assume that the sites for the quarries had been surveyed by the LGC and test quarries opened up to locate the best material. There is no evidence to indicate whether the tramway from the Main Platform was functioning prior to the opening of the quarries to provide access to the island plateau and on to the Landing Beach or gradually extended as the quarries were worked out.

In papers relating to the winding up of the LGC which are held in the National Archives, the three quarries served by the main tramway are named as Smith's Point Quarry, Middle Quarry and Howard's Quarry. On existing evidence it is reasonable to assume that Smith's Point Quarry is the northernmost, Middle Quarry is VC Quarry and Howard's Quarry is the southernmost of the three

There is very little evidence remaining to indicate how the quarries were worked, but photographs taken in the 1870s of mainland granite quarries in Devon and Cornwall give a very good idea of how the quarries on Lundy would have been organised (Stanier 1999). What can still be recognised in all three main quarries are the remains of the crane bases on which the huge timber mast-cranes would have been mounted. Ring bolts in the north and south faces of Smith's Point Quarry might well have been part of the fixings for the system of stays and guys that were used to stabilise the masts themselves.

The layout of the tramway that ran the length of the main workings from Smith's Point Quarry southward to the Main Platform is traced by the marks left after the removal of the granite sleepers (Figs. 44 & 51). These marks also suggest that short tracks led from each quarry to the head of the waste tips associated with it. The granite sleepers, along with all other removeable and saleable items, were sold after the Company went into liquidation. There are also the remains of what might have been a powder magazine or a latrine situated to the west of the tramway between the southern and middle quarries (Fig. 49).

Some way up the sideland between the tramway and the plateau, and running south from the south side of the northernmost quarry, are two crude terraces, one immediately below the other. They would have provided the track beds for short tramways similar to that which led from William Heard's Quarry and would most likely have been used to carry away the over-burden, rough waste and spoil from that level of the quarry workings. The upper of the two terraces, situated just below the granite outcrops at the top of the sideland, is the wider and better constructed of the two with an average width of two metres and extending for about fifty metres southward from the edge of the quarry.

The spoil tips associated with the main quarries bear further testament to the enormous waste of material involved in this enterprise. Even on the mainland, quarrying granite suitable for engineering and architectural work often meant that up to 75% of the material extracted was discarded (Stanier 1999, 79). Given the logistics of the LGC operation, the proportion of waste from the Lundy quarries would have been even more excessive. An expert in the economics of quarrying or mineralogy might be able to explain why this waste could not be used for sett stones, small building blocks or even hard core. One significant factor in the case of the Lundy quarries might have been the burden of the royalties due to Heaven under the terms of the lease, for the LGC had agreed to make payment for even the coarsest ballast. (See Appendix II)

The spoil tips are the most visible scars left by the quarrying and thousands of tons of rough granite remain as testament to the inefficiency of the industry. How many more thousands of tons of rock cascaded down the sidelands into the sea?

Fig. 47 : *The East sidelands showing the spoil tips associated with Smith's Point Quarry - 2008 (Peter Rothwell)*

The spoil tips and the size and quality of stone they contain are a valuable record and they, along with all associated buildings and works, have been scheduled as Ancient Monuments (Ref. 30352 - 30355).

The drawing (Fig. 45) illustrates how the Main Platform might have looked when the quarries were in full production. To the right are store sheds and open fronted workshops or bankers, where masons would dress and finish the stone.

It is also possible that a smithy was set up here to make and maintain the quarrymen's tools and equipment. If, as seems likely, horses were employed to pull the trucks on the tramway, they might well have been stabled here. If any specialist equipment for the working of the granite were used on the island, it would have been housed here. Recent finds on Quarry Beach suggest that the LGC were producing granite columns on the island although it is unlikely that these would have been turned mechanically. Two short lengths of granite column approximately 25cm in diameter have been found, one of which has a triangular socket in one end (Figs. 83 & 84?). If they do not provide evidence that such columns were manufactured on the island, then they must themselves be part of a piece of equipment that had been imported. Some finished granite was exported from the island as there were complaints of shoddy workmanship and faulty measurements from customers.

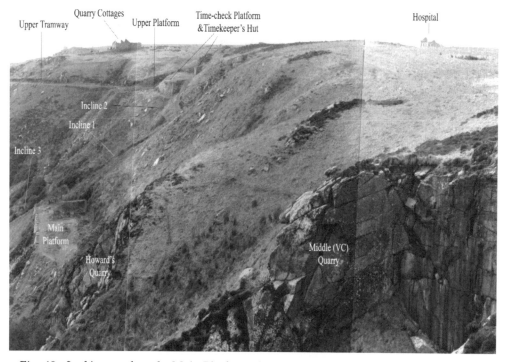

Fig. 48 : *Looking south to the Main Platform, the inclines and Quarry Cottages from Middle (VC) Quarry - 2008 - (Peter Rothwell)*

Fig. 49 : *Remains of a small building, possibly a powder magazine - 2008*
(Peter Rothwell)

Fig. 50 : *A section of granite 'sleeper' from the Main Tramway - circa 1960*
(Derek Sach)

Fig. 51 : *The Main Tramway looking north showing sleeper marks - 2008*
(Peter Rothwell)

Figs. 52 & 53 : *A pair of trolley wheels found in the quarry area - circa 1960. The gauge is typical of quarry tramways*
(Derek Sach)

Fig. 54 : *The Quarry Complex as it might have appeared in 1865*

when the quarries would have been in full production. (reconstruction - Peter Rothwell)

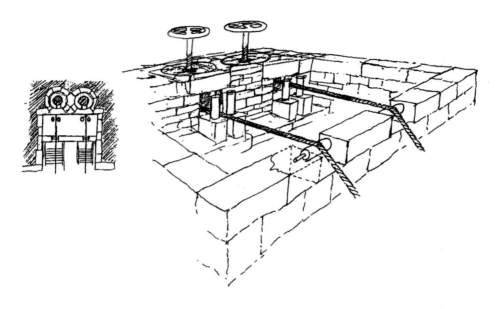

Fig. 55 : *Possible brake drum arrangement - (Peter Rothwell)*

Fig. 56 : *Remains of brake drums and 'Ratchet Steps' at the top of Main Incline - 2007 (Peter Rothwell)*

THE MAIN INCLINE

At the southern end of the Main Platform are the remains of the braking gear (Fig. 56, 58 - 60) that controlled the descent of the sleds or trucks to the Quay. It is not clear precisely how this system worked, so what is presented here is informed conjecture. The clues are:
- two openings for cables for each drum
- twin vertical guide rollers on spindles for each drum
- a single horizontal roller on the edge of the brake platform above the incline
- a pair of granite 'steps' at the head of the incline to act as ratchet brakes while the tub or sled is being loaded
- evidence on the incline itself of two pairs of timber rails approximately 20cm square and 1m apart, as shown on the 1886 OS.

Fig. 55 illustrates how the braking system might have worked if the above elements were brought together (the space between the rollers at the head of the incline and the drums would have been covered by boards and metal sheets). If, as is almost certainly the case, the system were gravity driven with the tubs connected by rope, chain or cable, the weight of the loaded tub or sled as it descended on one track, would pull the empty or partially loaded tub up the other. (Wire cable was invented in 1831). Once at the top, a ratchet brake on the tub would lock against the granite steps, automatically holding the tub in position for loading until released for the downward journey. How the braking system within the brake drums themselves worked is not clear from the remaining evidence. However, one possibility is that the drums around which the cable or chain was wound contained a mechanism similar to that employed in the 'drum and shoe' system, and operated by a worm gear controlled by the brakeman. It is possible that the brakeman's hut is indicated by the small square building shown at the head of the Main Incline on the 1886 OS map.

The tubs or sleds themselves were probably simple rectangular iron tubs, flat-bed trucks or sleds with stanchions on wooden runners, with guides that sat between the timber rails. One of the details that is not yet clear is the position of the tub as it was being loaded at the head of the incline. It would have been preferable from the point of view of those loading the granite for the tubs to be on the same level and horizontal plane as the Main Platform. However, this would have necessitated either that the rear of the tub be raised or that the tub itself be constructed so as to provide a permanently horizontal bed. The latter solution was employed, among other places, at the Vivian Quarry Incline in Wales (Fig. 61). It is probable that a similar if somewhat cruder solution would have been applied on the Lundy inclines.

Langham (1994, 176) suggests that iron rails were laid on timber sleepers. Two pairs of timber rails have been recorded but not the timber sleepers. However, in February 2000, latitudinal iron tie-bars, used to link and maintain the spacing

Fig. 57 : *Masonry laid over the track-bed of Incline 1 to support track of Incline 2 -2008 (Peter Rothwell)*

Fig. 58 : *Site of 'Ratchet Steps'at the top of Main Incline - 2008 (Peter Rothwell)*

Fig. 59 : *Remains of brake drums at the top of Main Incline - 2008 (Peter Rothwell)*

Fig. 60 : *Remains of brake drums at the top of Main Incline - 2008 (Peter Rothwell)*

between the rails, were identified and recorded (Figs. 62, 63 & 64). No evidence of metal rails has ever been found on the inclines and there would have been little point in going to the expense of laying metal rails, designed to reduce friction and make for easy running, when the greatest problem was how to slow the descent of the vehicle. Accounts describing the system adopted in similar inclines in Wales suggest that the timber rails had flat metal strips laid along them as had the skids of the tubs. What little remains of the wooden rails has been recorded but they will not survive very much longer. Clearly, a detailed survey of this section of the incline is vital before all the evidence is lost.

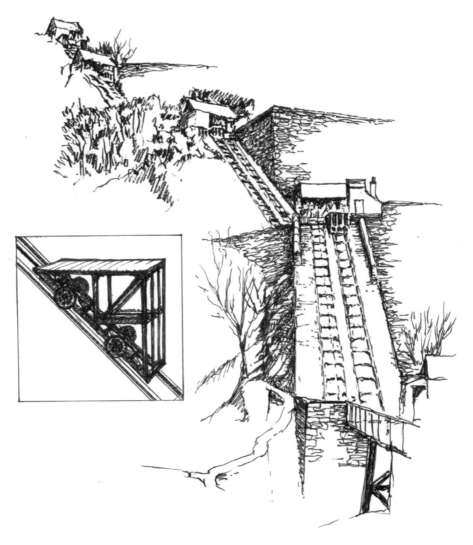

Fig. 61 : *Vivian Quarry Incline - Llanberis, North Wales -(Peter Rothwell)*

The beauty of the gravity system is its simplicity and efficiency, as it requires the minimum of mechanics, but it does prompt one or two questions about what happened at the base of the Main Incline. Anyone enthusiastic, or obsessed, enough to climb down the incline will realise that the steady gradient stops short by 30 or 40 metres of the level at which any quay or jetty would have been. At this point the sideland drops away much more steeply. Anecdotally, the theory was that the cliff had fallen away in the intervening one hundred years or so; this provided a very convenient and plausible explanation. However in 1997 a series of inclined terraces that zigzagged down the steep sideland at the point at which the Main Incline appears to drop away were identified and photographed (Figs. 65 & 67) thus disproving the cliff fall theory. These inclined terraces, each faced with rough masonry, could have provided access to the Quay and Jetty. They have since been recorded as part of the National Trust Archaeological Survey..

The 1886 OS shows the Main Incline extending to the Quay and an eyewitness account from August 1868 observes '...a tramway runs down to the beach.'(North Devon Journal, 20th August 1868). If this was the case and the inclined terraces were contemporary with the incline itself, it is possible that the incline was extended to the jetty across timber trestles (Figs. 66 & 76) and that the zigzag terraces are in some way associated with the supports for the incline or were used as a means of access during the construction work.

To obviate the need for an extended incline on trestles, it has been suggested that the tubs were slung beneath cables that stretched from somewhere on the sideland above the head of the Main Incline to an anchor point either on the jetty or on the beach or sea bed, There is no evidence remaining to support this theory and it does not explain the incline being shown as continuous from platform to jetty on the 1886 OS map (Fig. 69).

Aerial cableways were installed during the construction of the North and South Lights in 1896 and were used as a means of transporting supplies and material for many years. A cableway was suggested as a means of loading of granite and unloading of supplies in both the prospectus for the proposed Lundy Island and Mainland Quarries Ltd. in 1902, and Arthur Leon, in his survey for the Baron Rhondda in 1916, also proposed that a cableway be used. (see Appendices IX & X respectively).

What is also clear and remarkable...from both these documents is that, even allowing for the rather grandiose and over-optimistic claims made for the Lundy Granite Company in the original 1863 prospectus (Appendix VIII), and the very stiff competition from Scandinavian, Cornish and Scottish granite, not to mention the threat to further development posed by reinforced concrete, the professionals still considered the granite quarries to be not only viable but potentially profitable.

This conviction suggests that given proper management, marketing and investment, the exploitation of the granite resources of Lundy might have been a very lucrative enterprise indeed.

Fig. 62 :
*Remains of a timber rail
1960s - (Derek Sach)*

Fig. 63 :
*Timber rail and iron tie-bar
2002
(Peter Rothwell)*

Fig. 64 : *Pair of timber rails - 2002 - (Peter Rothwell)*

Fig. 65 : *Quarry Beach and Main Incline showing zig-zag terraces at the base of the incline - 2002 - (Peter Rothwell)*

QUARRY QUAY

The rather generalised map presented in Chanter (1877) (Fig. 69) shows a jetty sited at the southern end of Quarry Beach. This map appears to have provided the model for many of the subsequent maps and diagrams that indicate a jetty on Quarry Beach. However it is unclear from Chanter's map whether the jetty extends from the base of the cliff itself or from a wider structure which might in fact be a depiction of the quay.

The 1886 Ordnance Survey, published nearly twenty years after the closure of the quarries, resolves this issue as it shows a quay running northward from the southern end of the beach, roughly parallel to the line of the cliffs (Figs. 70 & 71).

The eastern face of the Quay is shown to have what appears to be a recessed section some 20m long which includes a set of steps built into the Quay wall providing a useful landing stage at high water (Fig. 69). During a search for the remains of the Quay foundations in 2000 a line of blocks was recorded, but not photographed, that related roughly to the general shape of the recessed section and was seen as confirmation of the outline of the Quay as depicted in the 1886 OS. This supported the contention as published in an earlier paper on the subject (Rothwell, 1999). However, current evidence indicates a quite different structure, for in 2006 no evidence survived on the beach to indicate the recessed section.

Either the original interpretation was mistaken or the foundation blocks have been buried beneath the mass of smaller granite boulders as a result of wave action. What was recorded in 2006, however, was a clear unbroken straight line of massive granite foundation blocks extending from the southernmost extremity of the beach for 100m northward that corresponds to the general north-south line of the Quay as shown in the 1886 OS.

The outline of the Quay on the 1886 map clearly indicates a well-defined structure complete with stone landing steps. We can assume therefore that the surveyors had observed such a structure prior to the publication of the map. However, it does not correspond to the evidence on the ground that was clearly visible in 2006. One possible explanation for the conflicting evidence is that in the years between the completion of the original quay in 1863/4 and the surveying of the Quay for the 1886 OS, the Quay suffered a partial collapse and was subsequently rebuilt incorporating the recess as a repair to the area of failure. A solid, stable working quay would have been vital if any further attempts to lease the quarries or export the granite were to be made. This could explain the two different profiles observed by the author in 2000 and 2006.

Allowing for subsequent erosion of the cliff, the quay would have been between 20m and 25m wide, more than sufficient to accommodate all the necessary services associated with a small port (Figs. 66 & 76). The quay would probably have resembled those associated with local harbours such as Clovelly and Ilfracombe or the granite quays of Cornwall. To handle the stacking and loading of the granite and the importation of equipment and supplies there would have been cranes, derricks, rails, trucks, storage sheds and docking facilities.

Fig. 66 : *Quarry Quay and Jetty - circa 1865 - (reconstruction Peter Rothwell)*

Fig. 67 : *Zig-zag terraces at the base of Main Incline (horizontal surfaces evident) - 2002 (Peter Rothwell)*

The granite, in whatever state, rough, part dressed or finished, would have been stacked on the Quay to await the arrival of the *Vanderbyl* to transport it to Highbridge in Somerset or to Fremington Quay on the River Taw some twenty or so miles away.

As has been suggested, many of the granite blocks that now litter Quarry Beach were once part of the quay itself. The fact that even its outline can still be traced to this day is a testament to the remarkable skill of the masons and engineers who were responsible for its construction. The total destruction of Hartland Quay, built in 1878, gives an indication of the immense forces to which Quarry Quay and Jetty would have been subjected.

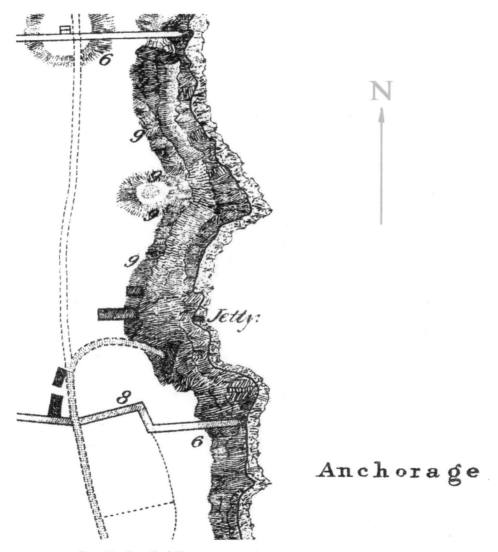

Fig. 68 : *Detail of Chanter's map showing the quarry complex - 1877*

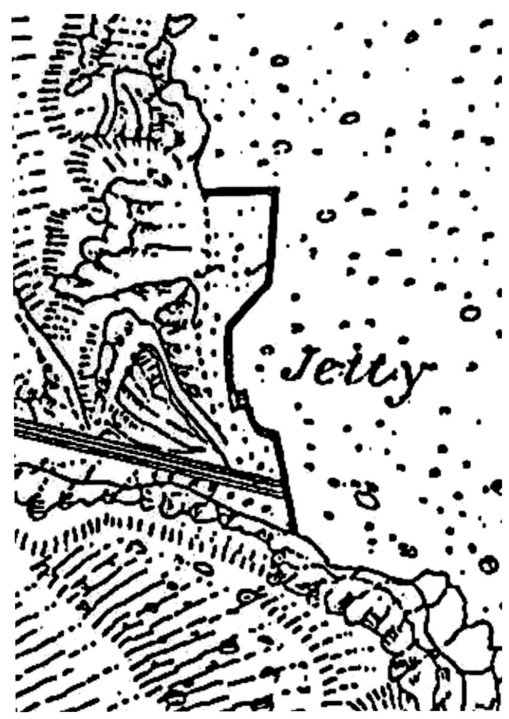

Fig. 69 : *Detail of 1886 OS map showing Quarry Quay and the lower section of the Main Incline*

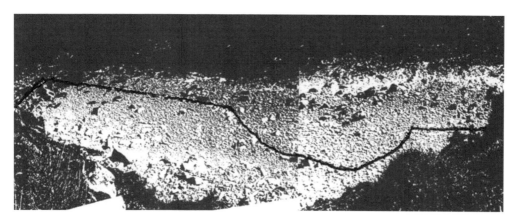

Fig. 70 : *Outline of Quarry Quay as observed in 2000 (line applied) - (Peter Rothwell)*

Fig. 71 : *Outline of Quarry Quay as observed in 2006 (line applied) -(Peter Rothwell)*

Fig. 72 :
Quarry Quay
foundation blocks
looking south - 2007
(Peter Rothwell)

Fig. 73 :
Quarry Quay
foundation blocks
looking north - 2007
(Peter Rothwell)

Fig. 74 :
*Quarry Quay foundation blocks showing connecting iron staple set in lead - 2007
(Peter Rothwell)*

Fig. 75 :
*Quarry Quay foundation blocks showing connecting staple - 2007
(Peter Rothwell)*

Fig. 76 : *Quarry Quay & Jetty as they might have appeared circa 1867
(reconstruction - Peter Rothwell)*

THE JETTY

In 2000, eight base blocks were identified, arranged in two rows approx. 12 ft. (4m) apart with each pair of blocks also approx. 12ft. (4m) apart. The blocks show the distinctive pattern of bolt marks (Figs. 77 & 78) that match the configuration of bolts fixing the iron base-plates that are still in place elsewhere on the beach (Figs. 81 & 82). The pattern of bolt marks indicates that the holes for the bolts were drilled in a square arrangement at 17 inch centres.

The problem as perceived in 2000 was that the lines of exposed blocks, being only four pairs in number, did not extend far enough eastward toward the sea to make berthing a vessel at the jetty possible other than during high spring tides. Even allowing for the likelihood that the granite boulders littering the beach are what remain of the debris of the Quay itself and that in 1863 the beach level would therefore have been lower, there would still not have been enough depth of water to allow a loaded vessel to float except during the highest tides. It was clearly an unworkable situation; the jetty would have extended further. The only likely explanation for the absence of the base blocks is that they have been moved from their original positions.

The mystery was solved during a detailed examination of the beach at low spring tide in July 2006, when every exposed example of 'dimension stone' (stone that has been finished to a given set of dimensions for construction work) was recorded. The search revealed another four base blocks. Two of these blocks had been only slightly displaced but one other was found at the extreme low water mark half-way along the north/south line of the beach, a full 100m from its original position. The last one of the four was situated on the high water mark at the southern end of the beach approximately 30m from its original position.

It can now be confirmed that each of the two rows of blocks was made up of at least six base blocks, giving the jetty a total length of approx 25m. As each block has four iron pins set into it in a square configuration they are clearly the base blocks onto which iron sockets or base-plates were bolted, and into which the timber piles for the jetty were set (Figs. 81 & 82).

Two of these sockets or base-plates with the same pattern of holes for bolts, but of slightly differing designs, still exist set onto the rocks of Quarry Beach. One, with a three-sided socket (Fig. 84), on a rock at the base of the incline in the extreme south west corner of the beach, some 2m above high water line (the remains of securing bolts arranged in the same pattern on the rock close to this base-plate, suggest that there was another plate approximately 1m slightly higher and to the south), and another, with a two-sided socket bolted into a recess especially carved into the granite on a rock in the centre of the beach (Fig. 81), adjacent to where the north east corner of the Quay would have been. There is also evidence of other iron fittings associated with this rock. It is possible that these fittings were for a mast crane erected to assist in the construction of the Quay.

As the jetty was of timber construction and even more exposed than the Quay, it is not surprising that once regular maintenance had ceased it lasted only a few years. A description of its sudden end is given in a letter from Cecilia Heaven to Hudson Grosett Heaven in January 1873, in which she makes reference to the fearful storms they had experienced on the island that winter, and,

> 'It blew from the nor' east. . .as for the jetty, it lies almost entirely on the beach.'
> Heaven archive

No boats had been able to land at Lundy for a month; not an unusual state of affairs. These circumstances give an indication of the vicissitudes that the islanders and the company employees had to endure. 137 years were to pass before a second jetty was constructed on the island. The jetty at Woody Bay near Lynmouth, although a later and more impressive structure, provides a useful indication of the type of construction that might have been used in the building of Quarry Jetty. (Fig. 80)

Looking at Quarry Beach now, it seems impossible that a vessel could survive grounding on the boulders that cover it. It must be remembered however, that the scene would have been totally different in 1863, and it is quite likely that the beach would have been of fine granite sand. In the far north-western corner of Quarry Beach there remains a small patch of fine white sand, which gives some indication of what the whole beach might once have looked like. The account of the visit made in August of 1886 describes the fine silver sand of

Fig. 77 : Jetty base blocks - 2007 - (Peter Rothwell)

Fig. 78 : Jetty base block - 2007 - (Peter Rothwell)

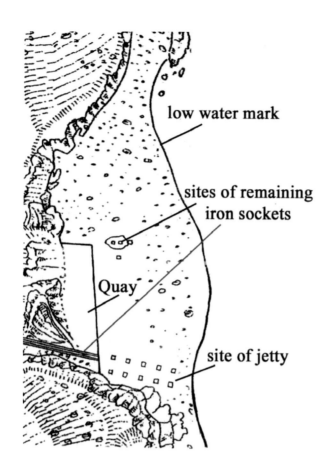

Fig. 79 :
Map of Quarry Beach
showing original
positions of jetty
base blocks and
iron sockets
(Peter Rothwell from 1886 OS)

Fig. 80 : Woody Bay Pier under construction- circa 1897 (Rothwell collection)

Fig. 81 :
Cast-iron socket
sited on a rock in the centre
of Quarry Beach - 2007
(Peter Rothwell)

Fig. 82 : Cast-iron socket - sited extreme SW corner of Quarry Beach - 2007 - (Peter Rothwell)

Fig. 83 :
*Section of turned granite column on Quarry Beach,
approx 20cm x 60cm - 2007
(Peter Rothwell)*

Fig. 84 :
*Section of granite column showing worked triangular socket - 2007
(Peter Rothwell)*

Fig. 85 :
Section of finished granite sill and 'stapled' foundation blocks - 2007 (Peter Rothwell)

Fig. 86 : *Section of wrought-iron rail - 2000 - (Peter Rothwell)*

pulverised granite on the Landing Beach glinting in the sun. If the Landing Beach looked like that, what might Quarry Beach have looked like? The waste from the spoil tips just a few hundred metres to the north being pounded by incessant wave action would have provided hundreds of tons of sand for these beaches.

On the cliff face immediately to the south of where the jetty would have stood are a number of drill holes and notched and levelled areas of granite. It is likely that these were the fixing points for some heavy pieces of equipment. The drill holes are all approximately 60mm in diameter and vary from 100mm to 300mm in depth. Evidence of iron bolts remains in several of them. It is possible that these mountings were part of a bracing system designed to reinforce the jetty against the force of a vessel pounding against its northern side. Alternatively they could be part of the rigging for a mast crane or derrick.

Of the large number of dressed granite blocks, 'dimension stone', on Quarry Beach, many will once have formed the main structure of the Quay; others will as certainly be parts of shipments that never made it off the island. Broken kerb-stones, window-sills and lintels can be found on the beach as well as the remains of granite columns (Figs. 83 - 85)

In 1999 a short section of iron rail (Fig. 86) was identified which is probably an off-cut cast aside when the track was being laid on the jetty. It was found, firmly welded into a large accreted mass of pebbles, hard under a granite block along-side one of the jetty foundation blocks. It is about 30cm long, 75mm wide at the base, 95mm high and the rail itself is 50mm wide. It is now lodged with the National Trust Archaeological Survey Unit.

It is the small, seemingly insignificant items such as this length of track that have provided some of the answers to the many questions concerning the work-ings of the LGC and enabled the facts presented here to emerge little by little from theories and speculations.

The establishment of the infrastructure necessary to support the opening of the quarries and the successful shipping of the stone, was a tremendous task demanding engineering and organisational skills of the highest order. The men who conceived, designed and constructed the buildings, the tracks and tramways, the inclines, the quay and the jetty deserved better support from those to whom they were contracted. The builders, masons and engineers did all that was asked of them and more. They were not responsible for the failure of the Lundy Granite Company. The fact that many of the buildings that survive on Lundy today were constructed by those same builders, masons and engineers is a testament to their hard work and a justifiable pride in their craftsmanship.

They were let down by the officers and directors of the LGC whose misman-agement of the situation on the island and of the Company's financial affairs was little short of criminal and brought about the inevitable collapse of the Company.

Fig. 87 : *A Heaven family outing on the Island - circa 1864 - (Heaven archive)*

THE END OF QUARRYING

By July 1865 it was reported at the AGM of the Lundy Granite Company that the works on Lundy had been set up, and that granite was in production with an average of one and a half cargoes shipped per week (a cargo consisted of 60 tons). The three quarries in operation, Smith's Point Quarry, Middle Quarry, and Howard's Quarry, and two mainland depots were established to connect with railway services at Fremington and at Highbridge near Bridgwater. This all sounded encouraging, despite a debt to the National Bank of £741 shown in the accounts. Mention was made of a contract for Dagenham Docks, but what was not reported was that the important contract for the Thames Embankment had not been obtained.

The debt to the bank continued to grow. In 1866 it stood at £6,579 19s 6d, and by 1867 amounted to £8,849 12s 5d. The balance sheet provided at the company AGM in August 1867 cited the expenditure as follows:

Cost of opening quarries, plant, machinery, jetty, tramway, and tools	£30,145 05 08
Expenses of the company to June 1865	£ 4,174 16 06
Farm stock, crops, implements, drainage, reclaiming land, building walls, out-houses	£ 5,283 05 01
Houses, offices, dormitories, beds, bedding, furniture	£ 5,334 11 01
Purchase & repairs to steamer	£ 5,286 16 05
Stock in hand, coals, tools, gunpowder...	£ 3,569 01 00
	£53,783 16 07

There had been a loss on the year's trading, which included one unfulfilled contract that had entailed not only losses but also a penalty of £600. The depot at Highbridge, having proved to be less convenient than the one previously established at Fremington, was relinquished in the summer of 1867.

At this point four of the directors resigned en masse, without explanation, and were replaced by one of their own nominees, which reduced the number of directors to three. The shareholders were so alarmed by the debts incurred without reference to an extraordinary general meeting, or any explanation, that they were galvanised into action. They appointed two of their number to work with one director, Vanderbyl, to report back on the dealings, and the prospects of the company.

North Devon Journal Herald, 20 August 1868

A party of excursionists visited Lundy from Bideford aboard the paddle steamer *Prince of Wales*. On their approach to the landing bay they saw the Lundy Island granite steamer, *Vanderbyl*, and later viewed the granite works.

The company have opened two quarries. The first of these did not appear to answer their expectations, the quality of the granite being rather porous. The second is of a fine quality, yielding a good polish when worked, and of a very close grain; it is stated to be everything that could be wished. The plant on the works is extensive, a tramway runs down to the beach, where a jetty is constructed for loading the granite, and all that appears to be wanted is a good market, and plenty of capital to work the quarries to make it a successful venture, the supply being almost inexhaustible.

*

North Devon Journal Herald, 1st October 1868

Lundy Island

'The Granite Works – It appears that the Lundy Granite Company are in course of having their affairs wound up. The company started about three years ago with a capital of £100,000. something about £80,000 has been called up and expended on works. . . the first working of the granite on the island was attended with considerable loss, from the softness of the quality; the quality recently produced has been of a superior quality and it is very probable that the work may go on under another company or the present one reorganised.

On Monday the whole or greater part of the hands came from Lundy Island to Bideford in a skiff, and at present the works are temporarily suspended.'

The two shareholders, Mr Adamson and Dr Owen, found the situation very far from encouraging. The books were not in order, nor were the records of transactions and receipts in place. The company had been run by the directors of the National Bank, most of whom were also directors of the Granite Company or their nominees. There was suspicion of complex concealed dealings between the directors of the Granite Company, the National Bank, and other companies using shared or adjacent premises. £5,500 had been advanced for the purchase of shares in the Weald of Kent Railway in the name of one of the directors, but no interest payments or any record of repayment could be found. Many of the shareholders - including some who were friends of the directors - were in arrears with payments on calls, but no measures had been taken to exact these, and the directors had allowed 915 shares (almost one fifth of the total) to be forfeited.

It also appeared that only one of the directors, Vanderbyl, had ever been to

Lundy and that just once. The accountant who had been sent to Lundy was a nominee of Joseph McKenna, who had brought him over from Ireland, as was the secretary, Costelloe, who crossed to Lundy every two weeks with the men's wages, and was another member of the National Bank staff.

The men on the island were often drunk and disorderly and it was complained that Ryan, the engineer, was continually drunk and abusive. It was perhaps inevitable that with some two hundred workmen, laxly supervised, on an island with very few sources of recreation apart from the canteen, there would have been fights, disturbances and damages. When one case came to Bideford court in 1865, the judge said that Lundy was:

'....*a refuge for the destitute. . . the fag ends of society.*' (Bouquet, 1963).

'Gray was farming for the Granite Company...

The end of the Granite Company was an anxious time, then, for their employees, fearing loss of wages, formed themselves into watchers, patrolling the island on horseback night and day to prevent their agents leaving the island, and the noise of the horses' hooves up and down the Beach Road and the challenging men at the Battlements was very disturbing at night.' Heaven archive

The failure of the directors ever to visit Lundy would have contributed to the fact that the configuration of Lundy and the difficulties of transportation had not been taken into sufficient account. On 19 February 1869 the *Caroline*, a sailing smack, was wrecked on the landing beach:

'Having loaded 43.5 tons of granite... left the shipping jetty at Lundy and brought up for the night in Lundy Roads. At 7 pm she commenced to leak, and by the time the wind had changed to N by E at about 4 am the following day, it was found that her pumps could no longer control the flow of water. It was therefore decided that the vessel should be run ashore, both to save the vessel and the crew. Six local men managed to get a rope on board, and pulled all the crew to safety.' (Larn & Larn, 1995)

At times another steamer, the *Ogmore*, was used, presumably under tender. (A 146 ton screw steamer, the *Ogmore* of Swansea, was built in 1866 for John and Alexander Brogden, railway contractors, coal and ironmasters, and land developers. On April 8th 1894 a steamship named *Ogmore* was wrecked on the Pembrokeshire coast near Milford Haven. It is likely they were one and the same).

An account in the 'Times' of July 18th 1867 reads:

'At the General Meeting of the Lundy Granite Company, summoned for yesterday, not a single member of the Board attended, and no business could be proceeded with.'

The next AGM was called for 21st July, 1868, although no report or accounts were available. It was later found that there had been a loss on the year's trading of £1,058 and the company's debt to the bank had risen still further. On the appointed day, at the stroke of 12 noon, two directors, the secretary and the solicitor entered the room where the AGM was to be held, and immediately resolved to adjourn the meeting until 20th August. They then withdrew before any of the shareholders was able to utter a word. On 15th August, before the adjourned meeting could take place, the National Bank petitioned for the winding-up of the Granite Company and recovery of the debt of £13,967. The shareholders were sent a notice of the cancellation of the postponed AGM, and they found that the bank had already nominated a liquidator, George Cape, and had made application for his official appointment. This the court granted on 28th August, having declined to hear the representations of the shareholders, who immediately appointed a solicitor to act on their behalf. They then made application to the Master of the Rolls for the appointment of their own nominee, George Whiffin, on the grounds that he was independent and impartial. This resulted in the appointment of both Cape and Whiffin as provisional joint liquidators.

The directors of the bank and of the Lundy Granite Company were doing all in their power to push through a rapid liquidation, but the shareholders were determined to get an impartial report, to refute the bank debt as having been incurred without due authority, and to revive the company. The shareholders knew that the Lundy Granite Company had never paid a dividend, the shares were unsaleable, and not one of the original promoters or subscribers to the Articles of Association of the company remained in possession of a single share.

The position of the Lundy Granite Company was becoming ever more precarious and by the autumn of 1868 the situation on Lundy was disastrous. There was no money to meet expenses, there were contracts pending and stone ready for shipping, but no ship or money to transport it, and there was no fodder to over-winter the farm stock The workmen were drunken, thieving, lawless and unpaid. It was estimated that the saleable value of the livestock would not exceed £1,000, and there were still workers at Fremington to be paid, as well as the quarrymen, farmhands and other employees.

The provisional liquidators sent Whiffin's clerk, Frederick Wilkins, to Lundy to make a report, but Mr Heaven told him that it was too dangerous to cross to the island as the quarrymen were not working, were armed and were raiding the stores. The engineer, Mr Ryan, was held to be an intransigent rabble-rouser, who led the workmen in refusing to allow any officials to land unless they were bringing the necessary £200 of wages money, so the Company secretary was sent with £100 to pay off some of the men. Strangely, he put Ryan in charge of matters on the island, and then arranged that the other men would be paid off provided they went to Bideford, which eventually they did. In September Frederick Wilkins was sent to Lundy to take charge on behalf of the liquidators.

Affairs in London were hardly more encouraging. Sir Joseph McKenna and three others were forced to resign as directors of the National Bank, following

> **Preliminary Notice of Sale**
>
> Messrs Boatfield and Hancorne beg to announce that they have been favoured with instructions from the Provisional Official Liquidators acting in the matter of the Lundy Granite Company (Limited), to sell by Auction a portion of the HORSES, CATTLE, SHEEP, and PIGS, belonging to the said Company, now on the Island, as soon as they can be removed to the mainland for that purpose.
>
> Detailed Particulars as to the time and place of Sale, and description of the stock to be offered will shortly appear.
>
> Barnstaple, Dec. 1868.
>
> *
>
> *The Barnstaple Times*, 8 June 1869:
>
> The Lundy Granite Co Ltd (in liquidation).
>
> 'The official liquidator of the above-named company is prepared to receive tenders for the purchase, in one lot, of the lease of the island of Lundy with the plant, machinery and materials used in the working of the quarries. Also for the farming stock, implements of husbandry, and other things connected with the farm and for the houses and buildings erected by the company with the fittings, stores, and household furniture and effects therein; and also for such stock of granite now raised as may be lying in the said quarries at time of sale; and also all other, the property of the said company, in the said lease, farmhouses, plant machinery, goods and premises (including the depot at Fremington). A printed statement of the terms and conditions of the lease and a description of the property to be sold may be obtained on personal or written application to Geo. Whiffin Esq., Official Liquidator, 8 Old Jewry EC, '

the exposure of their fraudulent trading of the bank shares. The matter was not directly to do with the Lundy Granite Company, but their connection with it would have been common knowledge in the city. At the hearing of the petition for the winding up of the LGC, it was referred to as:

> 'a puppet of the National Bank, the Lundy Granite Co, despite its name, was cover for a number of unsuccessful bubble companies and there is a suggestion that funds invested in the Lundy Granite Co. were improperly used.' (Slattery, 1972, 42-44)

Petitions were lodged by the bank and the shareholders. The shareholders contested the National Bank's claim of debts owed of more than £13,000 and made grave charges against the directors of the National Bank regarding the Lundy Granite Co. The judge said, 'the charges against the directors of the National Bank, or at least four of them, were that they had carried on a species of trade in launching and winding-up joint-stock companies for their own benefit; that in fact the National Bank *was* the Lundy Granite Co., that the debt

24th February 1869

Important & Unreserved
Sale of Horses, Cattle & Pigs
Messrs Boatfield & Hancorne
have the pleasure to announce that they have received
Instructions from the Official Liquidator acting in the matter of
the LUNDY GRANITE COMPANY LTD to
Sell by Auction at the Royal Exchange Inn
in Bickington in the Parish of Fremington, Devon,
on Monday the 1st day of March next, at one o'clock precisely,
the following LIVESTOCK which have been removed
from the Island for the convenience of Sale; consisting of
13 useful horses & colts, 37 Bullocks & Calves, 25 pigs.

The Horses comprise 3 strong cart mares, four & five years old; 2 Rowan Colts,
2 & 3 years old, an excellent match; 1 grey horse, 3 years old, a first-class cob;
1 entire cart horse; 1 grey gelding; 1 excellent grey pony, good in saddle & harness;
4 suckers.
The Bullocks & Calves comprise 4 useful cows in calf; 2 Barreners;
1 Devon Bull, two years old; 9 yearling heifers;
5 three year old and 11 two year old steers; & four calves.
The pigs comprise 1 Berkshire Boar; 6 large Store pigs;
18 good slips varying in size and age.
Luncheon will be prepared and on the table at 12 o'clock.

*

The Times 31 May 1869

'THE LUNDY GRANITE COMPANY (Limited), In Liquidation.

The official liquidator... is prepared to receive TENDERS for the PURCHASE, in one lot, of the LEASE of the ISLAND OF LUNDY, with the plant, machinery, and materials used in the working of the quarries; also for the farming stock, implements of husbandry...and for the houses and buildings erected by the Company, with fittings, stores, and household furniture and effects therein, and also for such stock of granite now raised as may be lying in the said quarries at the time of sale... including the depot at Fremington... the terms and condition of the lease, and a description of the property to be sold may be obtained on application to George Whiffin...'

> February, 1869
>
> The Lundy Granite Company
>
> Of the £100,000 share issue no more than 15,480 shares were allotted, since when a large number have been forfeited. At 15 August 1868 the number of shares in holding was 12,155. £3.10.0. had been called, leaving £1.10s.0d. uncalled.

claimed by the National Bank was illusory, and as such the shareholders of the Lundy Granite Co. were not legally liable to pay... he was of the opinion that there was matter of grave importance to be tried and that the conduct of the directors of the National Bank could not be conveniently or properly disposed of under a winding-up order obtained by themselves and carried out by themselves.' A winding-up order was made on both petitions, but the carriage of the order was given to the shareholders.

Meanwhile the debt to the National Bank had risen to £16,451 18s 4d. The deposits on the Shares taken up in 1864 were followed by four calls up to the end of 1866, but 1115 shares had been forfeited. Interest payments on short-term loans had been debited to the company, although the capital sums raised could not be related to company business. A contract to supply granite to the Admiralty at Chatham had been cancelled because the first consignment of stone was not delivered on time, and other contracts were lost because the supply of worked granite failed to meet specifications. In reports to the court it was stated that the secretary, Costelloe, had not paid all moneys received into the company's account, and neither had he paid for an elaborate monument he had ordered to be made and delivered to him and valued at £500. Indeed, the conduct of affairs had been so lamentable that it was suggested that the shareholders should sue the directors to secure recompense for their losses.

The battle over the appointment of the official liquidator went on, with the manager of the bank going so far as to lobby shareholders personally in favour of his own candidate. But on 19 November 1868 the Master of the Rolls gave the carriage of the winding-up order to two of the Shareholders In doing so he went so far as to remark on the -

> '...unsatisfactory and suspicious nature of the transactions between the National Bank and this Company. If the shareholders had not intervened, the whole matter would have been speedily settled in Chambers and the Lundy Granite Company would have been wound up after having made a considerable payment to the National Bank, but no examination in what appears to me very suspicious circumstances and which, in my opinion, ought to be carefully investigated.'

George Whiffin was appointed official liquidator in January 1869 and as he set about his work he complained that Cape had removed documents that he kept them on his own premises, and had been offensive and surreptitious. However, he persevered in his efforts to unravel the tangled and unsatisfactory affairs of the company. Some sheep and cattle were taken ashore and sold for £673, which also reduced the amount of fodder needed on the island. Heaven was owed arrears of rent and royalties, and the court authorised the liquidator to pay him £200 in April, £500 in July, and £297 6s 5d in October, out of Lundy Granite Company monies.

As well as outstanding wages, money was needed for stores for the men remaining on the island, for fodder for the animals, and seed for the farm. Although there were saleable stores of granite at Highbridge, Fremington, and at the London agent's wharf, charges were owed in all three places and none of the stone could be moved until the outstanding charges had been paid. Heavy dues were owed for the *Vanderbyl*, which was lying unused at Cardiff.

The valuer from Barnstaple estimated the company's saleable assets on Lundy to be worth £679, but advised that the plant, machinery and granite would cost more to move and sell than they would fetch on the market. £2,068 was owing to various creditors, apart from the debt to the bank. It should have been possible to raise some £18,000 with a final call of £1-10s on the shares, but the number of shares still in holding had fallen by 3,325 to 12,155, and it was probable that some of the holders would have preferred to forfeit their shares rather than payout more money.

George Whiffin's investigations were deliberately and constantly hampered by the destruction and withholding of documents, and obstruction by parties in alliance with the National Bank, but he uncovered some of the causes of the company's failure. Workmen on the island had been unsupervised and often idle:

> '...the business of the Company (there apparently being no system of management) being conducted with great irregularity. Upon several occasions there have been between 150 and 200 men on the Island and they have left off work for a week or two at a time, the Company being at the expense of their maintenance.'

Letters had been written to the Board by some of the servants of the Company remonstrating on the conduct of affairs in the Island but little or no action was taken, the Directors and Secretary throughout taking the part of Ryan (the principal officer on the Island).

The suspicious connections of the directors of the Company with the National Bank, and the involvement of both in other concerns not related to the company, were reflected in the irregular accounting and book-keeping, where transactions had not been separated. Both the administration of business and the management of the quarries had been seriously inadequate, and contracts had been lost either through late delivery of stone, a failure to deliver any stone at all, delivery of cut stone of faulty specification or from the unsatisfactory quality of the granite supplied. £3,000 had been an excessive sum to pay for a ship worth only a fraction of that sum, and no buyer could be found for it in March of 1869, even at the low auction reserve of £750.

The devious conduct of the Lundy Granite Company was made evident in a claim brought against it as early as 1865.

The Times, 16 February 1865.
Claxton versus the Lundy Island Granite Co.

This was an action for work and labour done by the plaintiff at the request of one of the directors of the company. It was desired to take granite from Lundy Island and ship it for London to be used for facing the Thames Embankment. Capt. Claxton went to the island and inspected it with a view of ascertaining whether it was possible to make shipping quays, and thus enable vessels to load granite from the quarry side. Capt Claxton had formerly been employed by Messrs. Brunel and Stephenson, and was engaged in…other works requiring the services of a marine engineer.

The defence was that Mr McKenna…had accepted the plaintiff's services on the condition that travelling expenses only were to be paid, and that the instructions given to Mr McKenna by Mr Hope, who communicated originally with the plaintiff, amounted to no more.

A letter was produced by the plaintiff, written to him by Hope, in which it appeared that the terms offered to the plaintiff were travelling expenses, and 'something for his time.'

The jury found for the plaintiff with damages.

Fig. 88 : *William Hudson Heaven in 1869 -aged 70 - (Heaven archive)*

HOPE REVIVED - A BUYER STEPS IN

It was at first an enormous relief when a buyer for the Lundy Granite Company was found in May 1869. He offered the very low sum of £4,000 for the entire concern, including the *Vanderbyl*, but it was the sole offer and had been secured with difficulty by Frederick Wilkins, whose commission was to be 5%. In his deposition dated October 1869 the liquidator referred to the lease as an asset of the Lundy Granite Company, as had also been clearly stated in the advertisement for the sale of the quarries. On the basis of the general assumption that this was correct, the sale was approved by the court. The shareholders and all parties concerned agreed that the sale was, without question, the best option available, and Heaven agreed that he would consent to the assignment of the lease on condition that he would receive payment of all rent arrears from the purchase money. At this stage it would seem that the complications of the situation were not appreciated by any of the parties, except the leaseholder, William McKenna. The lease had never been assigned to the Lundy Granite Company. Thus McKenna was legally liable for the arrears of rent and royalties and, to enable the buyer to take over the works, he would be required to assign the lease. He claimed that he had not been informed of the sale, though this was later disproved.

The buyer, Henry Benthall, was a contractor who owned quarries in Wales and, as he wanted to take advantage of the summer months to ship away the cut granite, the Clerk of the Court agreed to his having possession of Lundy from 24 June 1869. Benthall signed an undertaking to pay rent and royalties, and to fulfil the covenants of the lease from that date onwards, the draft assignment of the lease was to be prepared and sent to all parties for approval, the purchase moneys of £4,000 were paid to the liquidator, who in turn paid the arrears of rent to Heaven and to the railway depots, and Frederick Wilkins was paid his commission. On 24 June Benthall took possession and Frederick Wilkins, no longer employed by the liquidator, was installed at the farmhouse as manager, with his wife and two daughters. Edward McKenna was appointed as foreman of the works at a salary of £2 2s per week, with a rent-free house. He was one of the few to emerge from the debacle with any credit to his name.

The shareholders' affidavit presented on 29 November 1869 was damning. It revealed not only that William McKenna's lease had never been assigned to the Lundy Granite Company, but also that the contract for the supply of granite for the Thames Embankment had never been secured. Further, the state of the books and accounts was very unsatisfactory, and the appointment of directors irregular. The company had been run by the National Bank directors in their own interests and those of various companies with which the Lundy Granite Company shared premises (the offices of The National Bank were at 13 Old Broad Street, those of the Lundy Granite Company at 17 Old Broad Street and of the liquidators at 8 Old Jewry, all in EC2, within a stone's throw of each other and deep in the financial heart of the City).

> February 1869
>
> The value of the company assets was less than £3,500.
>
> The lease of premises at Highbridge [Bridgewater] had been surrendered to the lessors, Somerset & Dorset Railway, on 29 September 1867. One year later wharfage charges were owing for the quantity of granite that had not been removed. The granite was eventually sold at auction in Barnstaple, but the lessors would not allow it to be moved until the wharfage claim was settled.
> The company was also in debt for commission payments due to Samuel Trikett, of Victoria Stone Wharf in London. Granite had been supplied to the Dartmoor Granite Company, which took legal action against the Lundy Granite Company because the stone supplied was of inferior quality, and won their case. An order for stone for Surrey Docks was never executed, and other contracts were either not fulfilled, fulfilled incorrectly, or not to time.
> It seems the finest quality stone was taken from the north quarry, and was sent as sample in tendering, but that granite of inferior quality was sent in fulfilment of orders.
>
> The valuation of company effects for Benthall's takeover in May of 1869 was:
>
> | | |
> |---|---|
> | Furniture | £275. 0. 0. |
> | Livestock | 341. 0. 0. |
> | Dead stock | 53. 7. 0 |
> | Smith's and carpenters' utensils | 10. 0. 0 |
> | Granite, iron and steel | 673. 0. 0 |
> | | £1,352. 7. 0 |

As well as the establishment of the unnecessary depot at Highbridge, the ship *Vanderbyl*, expensive and unsuitable for its purpose, had been bought to support the candidacy of Philip Vanderbyl, one of the company directors, in the parliamentary election in Bridgwater in 1866. The election results were subsequently declared void. The writ (of election) was suspended and a Royal Commission was appointed, which reported that it had found proof of extensive bribery.

The seemingly happy solution of the sale to Benthall was overturned by William McKenna. As his lease had never been assigned to the Lundy Granite Company or to Benthall, he should have claimed payment of the arrears of rent and royalties from the Lundy Granite Company. But he would have known that the funds were not available and, as his involvement with the company was close, they may well have been working in conjunction. Frederick Wilkins claimed that he had secured an agreement with Heaven that he would cancel McKenna's lease and issue a new one to Benthall, and that McKenna had agreed, with unspecified reservations. Heaven later claimed that there had been no more than a conversation on the matter, and no agreement. McKenna then imposed conditions for the transfer of the lease with the idea of maintaining the extensive

Fig. 89 : *Old Broad Street, London EC2. Address of the National Bank & Lundy Granite Co. (Rothwell collection)*

advantages he had secured in the original agreement of July 1863 with the Lundy Granite Company. Further, he demanded an indemnity from Benthall of £5,775 in respect of the ongoing rents, royalties and covenants before he would agree to assign the lease.

During 1869-70, then, the situation was extremely confused. In summary: Benthall was in possession of the quarries and farm but was unable to work them without a lease, because the terms demanded by McKenna were impossible, which Benthall said left him paralysed. Heaven had refused to sign a lease until the rent arrears, which were accruing, had been paid. Benthall had borrowed the purchase money against a mortgage of the property from a George Rivington, who also claimed his interest. William McKenna as lessee, was legally responsible for the rents and covenants up to and after the Lundy Granite Company went into liquidation and until such time as the lease would be assigned to Benthall. Heaven had received no rent from Benthall or McKenna but, anxious to retrieve or renew the source of income, had omitted to exercise his right to re-possession for non-fulfilment of the terms of the lease. The Lundy Granite Company had no rights on the island, although it had enjoyed the benefits of the lease and was owner of the plant, machinery, tools and household goods still on the island.

Fig. 90 : *The Revd Hudson Grosett Heaven - circa 1864 - (Heaven archive)*

Frederick Wilkins, fixer of the deal, intent on his 5% commission, had either been ignorant, or had assumed from the advertisement that the lease was part of the sale, and had not reckoned on the complications that ensued. The Clerk of the Court had sanctioned Benthall's taking possession in June 1869 simply on assurances, without checking the security of a legally drawn-up lease signed by all parties, or even ascertaining the status of the lease.

Heaven, in need of money and anxious about the dilapidation of the farm, reached an agreement early in 1870 with Benthall, through Frederick Wilkins, to carry away some of the granite on the condition that he would receive agreed proceeds of sale either in cash or in farming stock, seeds and supplies. The Revd

Hudson Grosett Heaven, William Hudson Heaven's son, wrote to Mr Benthall in June 1870 to protest that as the proceeds had not been paid over, he would not agree to further shipping without proper accounting:

Lundy Island June 30th 1870

To H. Benthall

Dear Sir,
Mr Wilkins has been to me with reference to shipping away another cargo of stone, but I have told him I cannot in any way consent, in my father's absence, to allow any more to leave the Island till [sic] the money for the last cargo is remitted to the Island, or its equivalent in farming stock, seeds or other goods for Island use. It may be that without formal seizure we might find a difficulty, in a legal point of view merely, in absolutely preventing the removal of the stone; but I should certainly refuse to allow any assistance, as hitherto, being given by our men in the shipping of the stone, and if the attempt be made shall do all I can to get my Father to immediately make the necessary formal and legal seizure. In this I think he would be quite justified after the undertaking given by you to allow all the proceeds of the stone removed to be remitted to the island. It is not the mere idleness of the quarries that is in question alone, but the ruinous deterioration of the estate as a Farm which is going on at the same time for want of stocking and proper cropping and labour. The arable lands are now covered with a crop of weeds going to seed, sufficient to cause the expenditure of hundreds in labour for the eradication of them in future years. I am told that Mackenna [sic] (E. McKenna) receives payments every fortnight for the stone he delivers on orders. There can be no reason then why the money or its equivalent according to our agreement should not be remitted when the vessel comes for a fresh cargo from time to time; and then we would gladly facilitate the departure of the stone, believing it to be as much to our advantage as to yours that the stone should get into the market. But I cannot see that it is at all to our advantage that everything should go off the Island while not a pennyworth returns to it, and all on it is going to ruin. My father is in Bristol now and if you wish to communicate with him you had better write through his solicitors.
In much haste,
Yours faithfully.
H.G. Heaven

In this letter he appears to question Frederick Wilkins's trustworthiness which may well have been justified, since suspected French smugglers came ashore expecting to find him soon after his departure. The lengthy affidavit submitted by the shareholders entrusted with the winding up of the company in November 1869, confirmed that the Lundy Granite Company was controlled and managed not by its Board, but by the officers and nominees of the National Bank. £49,977 of shareholders' funds had been spent, and the current debt to the bank was claimed to be £16,451 18 04. Further, it was the shareholders' opinion that the money raised by the bank debts had not been used for the benefit of the company.

Lundy Island, July 14th 1870

To H. Benthall.

Dear Sir,
Mr Wilkins has handed me yours of the 12th and I am glad to find that we seem to be agreed in the interpretation of our compact.

I suppose Mr Wilkins will hardly require the full value at once of a cargo in store or goods, so I hope Mr McKenna [E. McKenna] will be instructed to bring a moiety of the value in cash, or at any rate a large proportion of it. We want labour badly in the Island both for saving the harvest and shipping the stone, but wages must be paid for labour and therefore cash must form part of the proceeds sent over. I am glad you have stated that the goods are to be invoiced, and allow me to suggest that a properly drawn up accounting of the value of the stone sold be sent with the invoice of goods and cash sent. There can arise no unpleasantness between the various parties, as to the actual equality in value between the goods and cash sent, and the cargo of stone previously removed. You know the general feeling on the Island regarding the trustworthiness of your agent [Wilkins] on the other side, and I am sure what I suggest will alone obviate squabbles in the matter.
In much haste,
Yours faithfully,
H. G. Heaven

William McKenna did not exercise his option to cancel his lease but he was very sharp in trying to manipulate the situation for his own interests, and in so doing he was responsible for the ultimate breakdown of the negotiations with Benthall. Heaven's solicitors wrote that

> 'it appears that Mr McKenna continues to act in a manner most detrimental to the prospect of an early resumption of the proper management.'

Without legal title, Benthall had not been able to take over the working of the quarries, and requested that instead of the assignment of William McKenna's lease, with the unacceptable terms, a new one should be drawn up. He wished to delete the clause in the existing lease that £700 should be spent on draining and fencing the farm, and to insert new clauses to...

> '...allow for the erecting of places of worship other than C of E, to allow cottages to be used for lodging houses, and to provide for the royalty payments for the granite to be calculated by measurement rather than weighing.'

Although Heaven was agreeable to the measurement of the stone, he was adamant in his refusal of the other terms, and wrote::

> '...to the building of Roman Catholic or Dissenting Chapels I would on no account consent. I cannot consent to any chapels. . . of any denomination except the Church of England being erected. I do not wish to debar anyone following his religion but I do not see why a room may not suffice for the purpose.'

Once again a draft lease was to be sent to the solicitors for all the parties concerned, but the situation drifted on without resolution. By this time Heaven concluded that Benthall would not be a desirable or reliable tenant, and he reproached Frederick Wilkins that he ought to have investigated the purchaser's credentials before introducing him. Frederick Wilkins replied that it was for each party to an agreement to satisfy himself about the probity of the other. The truth of the matter, which was not then apparent, was that Benthall was temporising because, after the long delays, he was unable to pay the rent or royalties that he had undertaken from June 1869. With no quarry income, he owed interest on his mortgage, as well as having the ongoing expenses on Lundy in wages, transport and running costs. In an attempt to resolve the situation, the liquidator applied to the court in April 1870 for an order to compel Benthall to complete his purchase.

> Transcribed from - Morris and Co.'s *Commercial Directory and Gazetteer*. 1870
>
> WESTWARD HO! is a hamlet of Northam parish, which has lately risen into notoriety as a new and charming watering-place; 2 miles north-west from Bideford, and 222 from London, by London and South-Western Railway, and 242 by Great Western Railway. It formerly consisted of a small farm-house, and a dining or pic-nic shed, known as Youngaton Farm, to which numbers resorted to enjoy a day on the beach and pebble ridge. In February, 1854, the first stone was laid by the Countess of Portsmouth, and by her named Westward Ho! . . .
> . . . the church was built by voluntary subscriptions, and is to be supported by an offertory, the seats all being free. The materials are chiefly from the neighbourhood; the stone from Kenwith and Westward Ho! quarries, the granite facings from Lundy Island, and tiles for the roof and flooring from the well-known Torridge Tile Works. The cost was about £1700. Mr. W. C. Oliver, of Barnstaple, was the architect, and Mr. J. C. Tremear the builder.

THE JUDGEMENT OF THE COURT

In 1870 judgement was given by the court that the Lundy Granite Company was not subject to any liability in respect of the terms of the lease or their agreement with McKenna, but that McKenna was at liberty to take his own proceedings against them. It was ordered that the contract of sale between the liquidator and Benthall should be rescinded, and the judge directed that the liquidator should supply the court with the following information:

> An account of all the property purchased by Benthall through the contract
> An account of all the sales and dealings made by Benthall of the assets transferred to him by the contract
> An account of all the rents and profits received by Benthall.
> An account of all the interest money on Benthall's payment of £4000.

It was ordered that any profits he had received from rent or sales were to be deducted from Benthall's £4,000 purchase money and the balance, plus the interest on the payment, was to be paid to him when he relinquished the island to the liquidator. Benthall was unable to provide the court with the information and accounts by the due date because Frederick Wilkins had not responded to his request for the necessary documents. In order to settle the matter the liquidator had to go to Lundy himself to fetch them.

By this time, exasperated and more than ever worried about the situation, Heaven took action in 1871 to distrain the possessions of the Lundy Granite Company as lien against the arrears, which by then amounted to £1,050. The liquidator obtained court orders to restrain Heaven from either removing or selling any property on Lundy belonging to the Lundy Granite Company, and the court also put the liquidator himself under a similar injunction. In the course of the proceedings it was stated that neither Heaven nor his solicitors had been aware of the agreement between McKenna and the Granite Company until after the company had gone into liquidation. In other words, they had continued to receive the rental moneys, but had not taken steps to clarify what McKenna's connection was with the Lundy Granite Company.

Heaven lodged an appeal against the injunctions that restricted his right to distrain, and the case was heard on 10 March 1871. The point at issue was whether Heaven was a creditor of the Granite Company or not. In what comes as a welcome breath of fresh air and sense in all this confusion, the appeal judges concurred in their opinion that since the debt was in respect of rent owed by the lessee since the winding up of the company, and since the company assets had been left on the island for the sake of securing a better sale for them, which deprived the landlord of re-possession, 'common sense and ordinary justice require the Court to see that the landlord receives the full value of the property.' Heaven was granted costs, the right to distrain, and to sell the assets if he did not receive payment of the rent owed from 24 June 1869 to 25 December 1870.

The moveable assets of the Lundy Granite Company on the island at that time were put at: worked stone £800, old iron £600-700, hay £200, plus 80 sheep, 6 cows, 1 bull, 4 draught horses and 3 or 4 donkeys, cranes and machinery, the railways, an iron building, smith's implements, and a large quantity of iron bedsteads and other effects. The farm implements were estimated to be so out of repair as to have no value. In April 1871 William McKenna relinquished the lease and the liquidator was empowered by the court to take possession of the assets on Lundy, Wilkins left the island, and Edward McKenna on Lundy was instructed to relinquish possession to Heaven. Although Benthall stated that he had not received any profits from Lundy, Edward McKenna testified that £101 19s 7d worth of granite had been transported and sold 1869-1871, but whether Benthall or the liquidator had directed this, or it was enterprise on Frederick Wilkins' part does not appear. Frederick Wilkins made a claim against Benthall for unpaid wages, stating that he had had a six-year contract from May 1869 for a salary of £100 a year until the quarries should be working, and £200 a year when they were in production. He stated that he had been on Lundy from July 1869 until April 1871, when the liquidator came to take possession, but that he had never received even so much as 1 shilling in wages Therefore he claimed £600 in wages, £49 for petty cash expenditures, less his store bill of £91 15s 8d making in all £548 13s 4d .

North Devon Journal, August 3rd, 1871

In Chancery
To Contractors, Engineers, Builders,
Stone Merchants, and General Dealers.

Sale of valuable Granite, Timber, Iron, Plant, and
Effects of the Lundy Granite Company Ltd. and
now in Liquidation.
Messrs Alexander, Daniel & Co will sell by Auction
by order of the Court of Chancery
at the Depôt, at Fremington, near Barnstaple,
on Friday next, August 11th 1871, a quantity of large
BLOCKS OF GRANITE; worked and rough,
including Steps and Curbs; various TOOLS;
AGRICULTURAL IMPLEMENTS,
Including Threshing Machine, Winnowing Machine,
and Horse Gear to work same,
a quantity of Timber, and other Effects.

In May 1871 the liquidator obtained the consent of all parties to remove the Granite Company moveable assets for sale by auction. Heaven refused to buy the granite, the plant, or the livestock, but agreed to leave the fixed plant in situ without rent so as to enhance the value of the quarries to any prospective purchaser of the works. The auctioneer sent to make the valuation reported that 'reprehensible neglect was manifest in considerable portions of the said effects from want of the most ordinary care... very extensively damaged, and depreciation in utensils and tools, and especially furniture, much of it fit only to be burned, rendered the loss to the company very serious indeed.' (see Appendix V) He estimated the consequent depreciation in the value of the effects, which ought to be charged against the person who had been in possession (Benthall) to be 40-50%. When the sale took place eight months later, the liquidator received only £659 7s after the deduction of costs for labour, and transportation of the goods from Lundy.

The consequence of the protracted proceedings that followed the winding up of the Lundy Granite Company was that the husbanding of the island had been neglected for the three years before the case was settled, and there were considerable losses and damage from deterioration, exacerbated by Lundy's exposed position.

The Times, 6 May 1872

'...Mr George Whiffin, the official liquidator... is authorised by His Lordship the Master of the Rolls to SELL by Tender, the whole of the PLANT, Machinery, and Effects of the above Company, upon the island of Lundy, consisting of wagons, cranes, slip and jetty, and quarry utensils, and also the plant and effects of the said Company now at Fremington Quay. A steamer will be provided for the conveyance from Ilfracombe to the Island of intending purchasers, free of charge, on the 9th day of May 1872 at noon, weather permitting...'

*

The Barnstaple Times, 8 June 1872

'The tender of Mr Councillor Down, merchant and general dealer, of Bideford, has just been accepted by the liquidators of the Lundy Granite Company for the purchase of the whole of the plant and machinery on Lundy Island.'

THE CLOSING CHAPTER

By May 1872 Henry Benthall was bankrupt, and his mortgagee, Capt. Rivington, recovered only £1,770 8s 7d of his £4,000 loan. It was found that despite the provision in the Articles of Association of the Lundy Granite Company that the directors were only to be paid fees from the profits, and none were ever made, the directors had taken fees, and the liquidator's application for refund was quashed on appeal. In the same month the liquidator gave evidence that £18,137 12s 8d of the company's debts had been approved by the court and paid, after a fifth call on the shareholders. He was directed to make another payment to the company's creditors, and the final total they recovered was ten shillings in the pound.

After three long years, Heaven recovered possession of the island, but he had lost the lease income, and was left with the farm severely run-down. At this distance, it seems strange to observe that the proposed lease to Benthall had in part finally failed over Heaven's absolute refusal to countenance any place of worship on the island that was not Church of England, although his age (he was 72), the worry, and his disenchantment with the whole peace-shattering enterprise were undoubtedly strong factors in his decision to take the island back into his own hands. What moneys he received in the final settlement, or from where, has not been found but they were sufficient to allow the purchase of a mowing machine, a new plough, and a haymaking machine after he resumed possession.

Lundy Island. May 11th 1872

To Mr Edward McKenna, Fremington.

Dear Sir,
My Father and myself have been talking over your proposal and on consideration he thinks it will be best to agree to your proposal regarding the Granite. The terms I believe are to be <u>cash down before the stone is shipped</u> for every cargo not exceeding 55 tons. This price to include large and small stones together not for <u>picked blocks</u> only. You are to be at the sole risk and expense of removal. We are willing to allow you the use of one cottage <u>unfurnished</u> for any hands you may send to do the work as long as we absolutely do not require it for our own use. You however must be responsible for any damage or injury of the premises beyond fair wear and tear during such occupation. As regards rendering any assistance in loading we cannot promise for certain to give it, but are willing to do so, provided our own work is not at the time such that we cannot without loss neglect it, and as I told you yesterday we are very short-handed and find even now a press of work upon us. Of course you would have to pay us for our men's time spared. My father also reserves the right to select and keep back any stone worked or otherwise which he may think likely to be useful to himself. He would also expect an advance in price for any worked stone you may wish to take away.
In much haste,
Yours faithfully,
H. G. Heaven

The whole of the fixed plant and machinery on the island was offered for sale by tender in 1872, and was bought by Councillor Down, of Bideford. The liquidator's final winding-up of the Lundy Granite Company dragged on, and was not completed until 1875, when the court order was made to:

> 'tear or cut into fragments all the books and papers and documents of the said Company except the file of proceedings so as to render them useless as a means of information and that such fragments should be sold and the proceeds accounted for.'

This leaves an unfortunate gap in the history of the company on the island itself, and, as the Heaven diary did not commence (or has not survived) until 1870, we know very little of the life of the Company personnel and conditions on Lundy. One odd footnote is that although Frederick Wilkins appeared to have utterly neglected the farm, he took it upon himself to apply to act as Registrar of Births and Deaths on Lundy during his period of residence there. This was the only time during the private ownership of the island that official or parish records of any kind were kept, apart from the census returns – for which Frederick Wilkins was also responsible in 1871. He described himself as 'Manager of quarries and farm of 924 acres and employing five men and one woman, Registrar of Births and Deaths '.

In 1869 an attempt was made to establish the Western Granite Company. Whatever the plan was it came to nothing for the company was never registered.

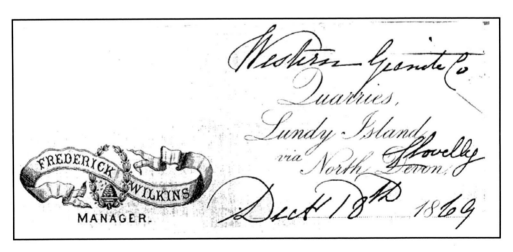

Fig. 91 : *Frederick Wilkins' informal letter-head for 'Western Granite Co.' - (Alan Rowland)*

Fig. 92 : *Smith's Point Quarry - posed photograph for LI&MQ prospectus circa 1902 (National Archives)*

Fig. 93 : *Smith's Point Quarry - 2006 - (Peter Rothwell)*

Although the Lundy Granite venture was not successful, Heaven had received a considerable income from 1863 to December 1867, and had the advantage of the reversion of a fine range of new buildings. These included the island store cum canteen (now the extended Tavern) that in itself became an asset, though the Heaven family avoided it themselves since alcohol was on sale there. In August 1872 the Court sanctioned payment of a further 3s in the pound which, with the previous payment, amounted to 7s, (Times, 1872). Other advantages had been the passenger transport afforded on the company ships, the delivery of some heavy supplies, and the presence of a doctor on the island. Although the family reserve was private and enclosed, the disturbance to the island was much lamented, and it is difficult to envisage the now tranquil island having such a large population, and resounding to the clamour of industry.

Attempts were made to revive the quarrying by speculators after a lease option was taken up in 1897, but several efforts to raise capital were unsuccessful and when he put the island up for sale in 1906, the owner (the Revd Hudson Grosett Heaven) cancelled the option.

In the best traditions of the island, in 1885 the material from the remains of the cottages that made up these accommodation blocks was recycled to provided the raw material for Lloyds Cottages, also known as Signal Cottages, and, tradition has it, the church of St. Helen. The contention is hard to accept, as the stone used in the construction of the cottages would have been very similar to the coarse, undressed granite that is to be found in what remains of Quarter Wall Cottages (Fig. 22 - Blocks G, H & I), Quarry Cottages and the Hospital. Since Signal Cottages were finished in brick, and all the stone used in the finishing of the church was dressed, it seems unlikely that the cottages provided any material other than a few dressed blocks or possibly infill rubble for the foundations and walls.

That part of the eastern lea of the island where the quarry workings were established has remained undisturbed and is now scheduled as a Grade II site. The granite works were at first seen as an eyesore, particularly the large waste tips. The extent of these is still remarked upon, but Stanier (1985, 183) comments that 'The winning of granite blocks suitable for engineering and architectural work has always necessitated the discarding of much rock, with as little as ten per cent of the quarried material being finally used'. The intervening 130 years have softened the contours of the shattered rocks and fostered trees and green plants, so the quarries today offer one of the most pleasant walks on Lundy, and the ring of heavy tools is replaced by the melodies of songbirds, the wind and the sea.

In contrast to the sorry story of the Lundy Granite Company, there is, in one of the quarries, a peaceful and fitting memorial to the courage and self-sacrifice of one of Lundy's sons, John Harman, who was awarded a posthumous VC for gallantry at Kohima in 1944.

Fig. 94 : *Middle Quarry (VC Quarry) - 1949 - (Ternstrom collection)*

AN AFTERWORD

by
Ann Westcott

It never seems to have occurred to the great melting-pot that was the new Victorian entrepreneurial class, that any influence could exist that might be outside their control - they believed that NOTHING was outside their control. For a very short time in British history, this astonishing capacity to ignore all difficulties made Great Britain the richest country in the world. The Manchester Ship Canal, Stephenson's *Rocket* and the Stockton & Darlington Railway, Cecil Rhodes' railway to link the south of Africa with the north, virtually everything that Isambard Kingdom Brunel turned his hand to, are examples of the almost casual brilliance of concept that could command funding from this new and increasingly powerful class.

William Hudson Heaven himself might be the only person of whom it could be said that he was influenced by events he could not control. His financial position in the 1830s was due in part to a new idea (that the Slave Trade was immoral) breaking through centuries of acceptance of an old idea, and destroying that acceptance.. The Slave Trade ('a thoroughly respectable trade') vanished (for Englishmen) in 1833 when Act of Parliament abolished it. William Hudson Heaven needed urgently to supplement his dwindling income, but, he was, perhaps, too absorbed in the old notions of gentility, too 'Establishment' ever to be a member of this new entrpreneurial class, he was not a Nonconformist.

The mid-17th Century until the early 20th Century was a time for the Nonconformist to turn his hand to trade. A Nonconformist (William Hudson Heaven called them 'Dissenters') was a person who did not belong to the controlling Church of England - the Catholics, the Jews, the Methodists, the Quakers, the Baptists, and many numerically smaller Religious Groups whose beliefs prevented them from following the Anglican (Church of England) rules, were unable to enter any Profession. All professional routes to income were closed to them by Act of Parliament - so the Frys, the Wills, the Rowntrees, the Cadburys, the Rothschilds, the Strutts and the Wedgewoods and their like, joined the new entrepreneurial class. Their abilities and dedicated management, not only established them as household names, but gave them power and influence. William Columban McKenna, a Catholic, was interested in power and influence. He saw the commercial potential of Lundy granite and set out to exploit it.

William Columban McKenna's character, 'impulsive and restless...' and inherently antagonistic to authority, (See Colley, Appendix XII), and his experience as a Surveyor of Stamps & Taxes (cf today's Inspector of Taxes) enabled him to embrace the ethics of the new entrepreneurial class as William Hudson Heaven was not able to do. William Columban McKenna was closely acquainted with influential members of this new class. His brother, Joseph Neale McKenna was an MP and Chairman of the National Bank of Ireland, later to become the National Bank, (which was to be the Banker for the Lundy Granite Company). Having secured the lease, William Columban McKenna made an 'arrangement' with his brother, Joseph Neale McKenna, who had set up the Lundy Granite Company, to sell the quarrying rights to the Company.

Clearly there are risks attaching to the launch of any new enterprise, but William Columban McKenna's method of securing himself against risk was unusual. Although the lease was drawn up between William Columban McKenna and William Hudson Heaven, the Lundy Granite Company operated the quarries according to the terms of that lease, without the lease ever being assigned to the Company by McKenna. He was never a Director. He was never a Shareholder. He never, as it were, took Centre Stage. But, at the same time, he never shared his tenancy with anyone. All its privileges remained his, and he appears never to have honoured any of his obligations as a tenant. When one attempts to see who suffered from William Columban McKenna's scheming and the Lundy Granite Company's entrepreneurial greed, actual 'victims' are hard to find. William Hudson Heaven was not one of them. He eventually emerged with the rental arrears paid up and, apart from the run down farm, substantial improvements to the island's assetts. The quarry employees were eventually paid off and even the sharholders recouped some of their money - probably as much as they could expect today under similar circumstances. Commercial ethics do not appear to have changed much since 1868. A share gamble remains a share gamble, and Trade Unions still provide a necessary protection. The first Trades Unions, however, (c 1831), might not have been much help to the quarrymen... 'the charges against the Directors...were that they had carried on a species of trade in launching and winding-up joint-stock companies for their own benefit... there was matter of grave importance to be tried... .'

The achievements on the island of the men who created the buildings and the structures which made up the fully-functional quarry complex are, without doubt, the most impressive outcomes of the whole enterprise. If the Directors of the Lundy Granite Company deserve any credit at all, it is because they appointed an engineer and a quarry manager who had the gift of making a team from 'the fag ends of society'. The fact that the quarry complex and its infrastructure were brought into being at all, is to their sole credit, not to the credit of any member of the Board of Directors of the Lundy Granite Company.

In the years between 1863 and 1868 all construction work on the Island from the Farmhouse to Halfway Wall was undertaken by the men of the Lundy Granite company, directed, not by any member of the Board of Directors, but by the engineer (Ryan) and the quarry manager, and Ryan was called a 'rabble-rouser', by the entrepreneurs. Yet the achievements of the skilled builders, masons and quarrymen demonstrate, as Leon was later to explain to Baron Rhondda (see Appendix X) that the potential for commercial quarrying on Lundy was immense. And it was still being explored as late as 1922, (See Appendix XV). BUT if that potential were to be fully realised, there also HAD to be in place dedicated Management - a skill singularly little exercised by any Director of the Lundy Granite Company.

It is ironic that the, perhaps, most satisfying outcome of the whole enterprise is the eventual triumph of fair play. The manoeuvrings of William Columban McKenna and the Directors of the Lundy Granite Company gave rise to a legal judgement, which states that a landlord may distrain goods left on his land- whether belonging to a tenant or not. This principle is enshrined in our Law (see Appendix VI) And as a result, making the sort of 'arrangement' that William Columban McKenna made with his brother, Joseph Neale McKenna, is now very difficult, if not impossible, to bring off.

It is of striking interest that, in a small and undeveloped island, there occurs, almost with the perfection of a fossil, the record of a continuum of Man's effect on his landscape, from the Upper Palaeolithic to the Present Day - some 13,000 years. The whole period of commercial quarrying is only one brief moment of this continuum, which, thanks to the National Trust, Sir Jack Haywood, Sir John Smith and the Landmark Trust, can still be explored 'on the ground', and thanks to the Research Work of amateur archaeologists and historians like Peter Rothwell and Myrtle Ternstrom, the evidence that remains of this fascinating episode can be more fully understood and shared.

Fig. 95: *Sir Joseph Neale McKenna - circa 1867*
(National Archives)

APPENDICES

APPENDIX I	p. 113	Summary of Persons
APPENDIX II	p. 115	Extracts from the Heaven - McKenna lease of 1863
APPENDIX III	p. 129	WH Heaven's correspondence regarding the marketing of Lundy Granite.
APPENDIX IV	p. 134	Miscellany of extracts and cuttings
APPENDIX V	p. 140	Inventory of the Deficiencies in Assets on Lundy 1868
APPENDIX VI	p. 143	A Legal Precedent
APPENDIX VII	p. 149	1871 Census Returns for Lundy
APPENDIX VIII	p. 154	Prospectus of The Lundy Granite Co. Ltd.
APPENDIX IX	p. 159	Prospectus of The Lundy Island & Mainland Quarries Ltd.
APPENDIX X	p. 164	Leon Survey for Baron Rhondda -1916
APPENDIX XI	p. 170	Dr. A. T. J.. Dollar's map of the geology of Lundy
APPENDIX XII	p. 171	Extract from 'Railways and the mid-Victorian income tax', by Robert Colley
APPENDIX XIII	p. 174	The text of a statement issued by Samual Griffiths regarding the Election of 1865 in the Borough of Wolverhampton with refernces to Philip Vanderbyl.
APPENDIX XIV	p.175	Interview with Tim Marsh.

*

APPENDIX I

Summary of Persons
(in alphabetical order)

HENRY BENTHALL
A contractor who bought the quarries, with all the plant and assets on Lundy, including the *Vanderbyl*, for £4000 in June 1869. He took possession, but did not secure the lease or operate the works, and the sale was rescinded by court order in January 1871. Only a portion of the purchase cost was recovered, and that was owed to Benthall's mortgagee, so that Benthall was left bankrupt.

GEORGE CAPE
Candidate for the post of liquidator proposed and supported by the directors of the National Bank. Given provisional appointment jointly with George Whiffin 19 November 1968 until 29 January 1869.

FRANCIS COSTELLOE
Secretary of the Lundy Granite Company.

WILLIAM HUDSON HEAVEN
1799-1883, owner of Lundy from 1836.

THE REVD HUDSON GROSETT HEAVEN
1826-1916, eldest son of William Hudson Heaven,

EDWARD McKENNA
Was appointed manager of the Lundy Granite Co. depot at Highbridge (Bridgewater) in 1866, and then Fremington. In June 1869, when the granite quarries were sold to Benthall, he was appointed foreman of works on Lundy in July of 1869. Prior to the sale to Benthall, he assisted with the valuation of the plant, farm, stock, and assets of the Lundy Granite Company, and carried out the same work in 1871 when the sale to Benthall was rescinded. He also attested the details of removal of granite for sale during Benthall's occupation.

SIR JOSEPH NEALE McKENNA, MP
Brother of William, and chairman and director of the National Bank. On 18 July 1863 he established the Lundy Granite Company, of which he was also director. A contract had been made with his brother, William, on 10 July 1863 for the sale and transfer of the lease of Lundy to the company, which was not fulfilled..

WILLIAM COLUMBAN McKENNA
A financial agent and some time Surveyor of Taxes, undertook the lease of Lundy and the right to take granite, August 1863. He effectively prevented the continuation of the quarry works by his refusal to surrender the lease.
Father of Reginald McKenna who went on to become Chancellor of the Exchequer to the Asquith coalition Government in 1915.

GEORGE RIVINGTON
Advanced the purchase money for the granite works to Benthall by mortgage. He recovered only part of his capital.

PHILIP VANDERBYL, MP
A director of the Lundy Granite Company. The only one of the directors of the LGC ever to visit Lundy. The establishment of the depot in Highbridge was intended to support his candidacy for a seat in Bridgwater in the general election of 1868. Election of Vanderbyl was declared void. The writ (of election) was suspended and a Royal Commission was appointed, which reported that it had found proof of extensive bribery.

GEORGE WHIFFIN
Provisional joint liquidator on behalf of the shareholders with George Cape until 29 January 1869, when he was appointed as official liquidator.

FREDERICK WILKINS
Clerk to George Whiffin, was sent to Lundy as overseer in September 1868. He secured the offer to buy from Benthall, and from June 1869 he remained on Lundy as his manager. When the court rescinded the sale, he was retained as the liquidator's representative on the island until the lease to William McKenna was terminated in April 1871. While on the island he was, by his own application for the post, Registrar of Births and Deaths. His *bona fides* were suspect.

*

APPENDIX II

Extracts from the Heaven - McKenna lease of 1863

...August one thousand eight hundred and sixty three between the Reverend George Williams of Ludmore House in the parish of Minchin Hampton in the county of Gloucester clerk, and Mary Williams his wife and Caroline Helps Morris of the same place spinster mortgagees in fee of the hereditaments hereinafter described and intended to be hereby demised of the first part William Hudson Heaven of the Island of Lundy in the Bristol Channel, Esquire, mortgagor in fee of the same hereditaments of the second part and William Columban McKenna of Number 8 Colville Terrace, West Bayswater in the County of Middlesex, Esquire of the third part witnesses that in consideration of the rent and the covenants hereinafter reserved and contained and on the part of the said William Columban McKenna ... to be paid, observed and performed, they the said George Williams, Mary Williams and Caroline Helps Morris with the approbation of the said William Hudson Heaven do and each of them doth hereby demise and dispose of and he the said William Hudson Heaven doth hereby demise and confirm unto the said William Columban McKenna... all that the Island of Lundy situated in the Bristol Channel foresaid and partly derivated by way of further description but not of restriction in the plan endorsed upon the second skin of these presents with the rights, easements and reputed appurtenances and thereto belonging but except hereinafter excepted and with the reservations hereinafter contained together with a way of grant and not of exception for liberty and power for the said William Columban McKenna... and his and their agents, miners, workmen, and servants at all times during the term hereby granted to dig, search for and quarry granite porphyry and other stone applicable for building or architectural purposes in or under the land hereby demised and dress make marketable and carry away and sell the same and to erect and from time to time alter or remove all such building: steam engines and machinery and to lay down and use all such railways, tramway and other roads and ways and to employ all such other means as shall be found necessary and expedient for the purpose of digging, searching for and quarrying the said granite porphyry and such other stones as aforesaid and making such marketable and carrying away the same but so nevertheless that no building erected by the said William Columban McKenna... for the purpose of or in connection with any of the quarries worked in pursuance of these presents shall be removed by him or them during the last year of the term hereby granted or after the expiration of the same term if nevertheless and except out of these presents all such parts of the said Island and all such easements and privileges as have been demised for the Corporation of the Trinity House of Deptford Strand and also except and always reserved unto the said several persons, parties hereto of the first part... and unto the said William Hudson Heaven... all such parts of the said Island as are coloured green on the said plan and the place called Benjamin's Chair with two acres of land around the same to the south of the Trinity Road and west of the short wall fence of upper Castle Hill and also the site of the Chapel near the Lighthouse and the burial ground thereto adjoining lands full right and liberty to enter upon and use for all purposes besides the part coloured green on the said plan and reserved as aforesaid all other land next to the sea round the whole of the said Island to the extent of ten yards above high water mark measured in a horizontal direction provided such last mentioned right and liberty be not used as to prevent the said William Columban McKenna. . . from landing thereon or quarrying stone therefrom or shipping the same therefrom, but by way of grant and not or exception with full liberty for the said William Columban McKenna. . . to use in common with the said several persons parties hereto of the first part. . . and the said William Hudson Heaven. . . and other persons entitled here the landing place marked on the said plan and the several roads from the Quay to the interior of the said Island the said William Columban McKenna. . . keeping the said roads in good repair and condition and also with full liberty for the said William Columban McKenna. . . at his or their own expense if he or they shall consider proper to consort or build for his and their own private use and for facilitating the shipping of the produce of the quarries hereby authorised to be opened and of the farm hereby demised but not for any public purpose or any other purpose than as aforesaid a harbour, pier or breakwater at or near Gannets Combe towards the north-eastward end of the said Island or at any other part of the coast of the said Island except that coloured green on the said plan and also to build a church or chapel in which the services of the Church of England only shall be performed and also a school-room and reading-room and also are messuages or buildings which he or they may consider necessary for the residence of himself or themselves or of any of his or their workman or agents employed in the said Island or for the use or accommodation of any person or persons coming to the said Island for the bonafide purpose of purchasing any of the granite porphyry stone or any farming produce quarried or produced on the said Island or for the use accommodation of any person or persons having an interest in the said farm and quarry or for the sale therein of the said produce or of any property or goods imported in the said Island for the supply of the workmen or other persons connected with, employed on or having an interest in the works or farm supposed to be carried on so nevertheless that the said pier or breakwater or improvements in the said harbour and all such messuages and buildings as aforesaid shall be constructed made and built in a workmanly manner and during the term hereby granted be kept in good order and repair by and at the expense of the said William Columban McKenna. . . and also except and always observed unto the said several persons, parties hereto of the first part their. . . and unto the said William Hudson Heaven. . . all mines and minerals including slate in or under the land hereby demised or any part thereof other than the said granite porphyry and other stone applicable for building or architectural purposes with power for the said several persons parties hereto of the first part their. . . and the said William Hudson Heaven. . . at any time or times to enter upon the hereby demised premises or any part thereof with workmen, miners and others to search for said excepted mines and minerals and to open and work the same and to carry away and dispose of for their and his own use the produce thereof and for such purposes or to erect and from time to time remove all such buildings, steam engines and other machinery as they or he shall think expedient and to make and use all such railways, tramways and other roads or lays and to do all such acts and things as shall be necessary or expedient for searching, for working, winning, washing, dressing and making marketable and carrying away the said excepted mines and minerals or any of them making nevertheless from time to time except in the cases where it is hereby expressly stated that no compensation is to be made reasonable compensation to the said William Columban McKenna . . . for the damage occasioned to the surface of the hereby demised premises by the exercise of any of the foresaid rights, privileges and easements in relation to the said excepted mine and minerals but so that no compensation shall be claimed by reason of damage done to the surface by any roads or tramways which shall be made for the purposes of the said excepted mines and minerals or for carrying away the produce thereof and also except and always reserved unto the said several persons, parties hereto of the first part . . . and unto the said William Hudson Heaven his heirs and assigns full power at any time or times and without making any compensation or any abatement rent in consequence thereof to enclose and plant with trees and shrubs any part or parts of the land hereby demised which they or he may reasonably think fit with free access to and from such part or parts for the purpose of enclosing and planting the same and preserving and promoting the growth of the trees and shrubs aforesaid and also except and always reserved unto the said several persons, parties hereto of the first part. . . and unto the said William Hudson Heaven. . . full power at any time or times without making any compensation or any abatement of rent in consequence thereof to take and enclose any part or parts of the land hereby demised not exceeding in the whole ten acres and not being within one hundred and fifty yards of the house marked on the said plan, farm house or of any house then erected or in the course of erection by the said William Columban McKenna. . . consistently with these presents on the said demised premises which they or he may consider expedient for the purpose of more conveniently working the said excepted mines and minerals and exercising any of the powers and privileges hereby reserved in relation hereto and to use such enclosed for such purposes accordingly and also except and always reserved under the said several persons, parties hereto of the first part their. . . and unto the said William Hudson Heaven . . . all such land not exceeding thirty acres in the whole to the south of the wall marked quarter wall on the said plan and not exceeding sixty acres in the whole to the north of the same wall as the said several persons, parties hereto of the first part. . . or the said William Hudson Heaven. . . shall think fit to enclose or take for the purpose of building thereon or on any part on parts thereof a dwelling house or dwelling houses or other buildings and laying out the same or any part or parts thereof as gardens and pleasure grounds or for any other purpose with free and uninterrupted access to and from such excepted land at all times and by all reasonable ways and means making nevertheless in respect of land so enclosed or taking as last aforesaid a reasonable deduction for the annual surface a rent of £500 hereby reserved the amount of such deduction to be determined a case of dispute by the Mayor for the time being of BIDEFORD in the County of Devon, but so nevertheless that the reservation lastly herein before contained shall not authorise the said several persons, parties hereto of the first part...... or said William Hudson Heaven. . . to take any land on which the said William Columban McKenna. . . shall consistently with these presents have previously erected or bonafide or commenced erecting any building of the value of £100 or upwards nor to take any land on which the said William Columban McKenna. . . shall have erected or on bonafide have commenced erecting any building of less value than £100, unless upon payment to the said William Columban McKenna. . . of the value of such building such value in case of dispute to be determined by arbitration as hereinafter provided and also except and always reserve unto the said several persons, parties hereto of the first part their. . . and unto the said William Hudson Heaven. . . full power and liberty to quarry and take granite porphyry or other stone in any part of the hereby demised land, but so as not unnecessarily to interfere with the works of the said William Columban McKenna... for the purpose of building any house or houses or any other buildings or walls in or upon any of the lands hereby reserved to the said several persons, parties hereto of the first part... and the said William Hudson Heaven... or which they are hereby respectively authorised to enclose or take as aforesaid and also except and always reserve unto said several persons, parties hereto of the first part... and unto the said William Hudson Heaven... all game and wild fowl and the sole and exclusive right of shooting and sporting over the said Island with the liberty of ingress, egress and regress to and for the said several persons, parties hereto of the first part... and the said William Hudson Heaven... and their and his friends, companions, game-keepers, agents and servants at all times in the year to shoot, course, fish, fowl and sport in and over the said demised premises or any part thereof and also to walk and ride in and over the same premises or any part thereof at any time or times for recreation pleasure and for all other purposes and also except and always reserved unto the said several persons, parties hereto of the first part... and unto said William Hudson Heaven... full right and liberty for them and him and their and his friends, agents and servants to gather eggs and mushrooms in all such parts of the said Island as are hereby demised for their and his own use, but not for the purpose of sale and also except and always reserved unto the said several persons, parties hereto of the first part... and unto the said William Hudson Heaven... the full right and the liberty of using in common the said William Columban McKenna his heirs... all roads and paths in such part of the said Island as are hereby demised and also except and always reserved unto the said several persons, parties hereto of the first part... and unto the said William Hudson Heaven... the sea fishery of all belonging to the said Island all the royalties, escheat, wrecks, jetsams, waifs, treasure trove and other manorial rights and privileges in and upon the said Island and premises or appertaining thereto and all such rights and powers as shall be necessary or expedient for giving full effect to the several exceptions and reservations herein before contained so nevertheless that the rights powers, easements and privileges hereby reserved to the said several persons, parties hereto of the first part... to the said William Hudson Heaven... shall be so used and exercised as not cultivating the land hereby demised or from working and quarrying the said granite porphyry and other stone which he and they are authorised by these presents to work and quarry on any part of the land hereby demised which shall not at the time being have been taken or enclosed by the said several persons, parties hereto of the first part... or the said William Hudson Heaven... in pursuance of the powers and reservations hereby reserved to them and to have and to hold all and singular the hereby demised premises unto the said William Columban McKenna... for the term of fourteen years from the twenty ninth day of September one thousand eight hundred and sixty three yielding and paying therefore yearly and every year during the said term the yearly rent of five hundred pounds as surface rent for the said premises and also yielding and paying yearly and every year during the said term in addition to the said surface rent the certain yearly rent of two hundred pounds to be payable whether any granite porphyry or other stone shall be gotten or not out of the hereby demised premises and also yielding and paying yearly and every year during the said term for all granite porphyry and other stone which shall be gotten and carried away from the said Island in pursuance of these presents or which shall be employed on the said Island for any public works or for any other works or buildings or purposes and except as is otherwise expressly provided by the proviso next hereinafter contained the royalties following that is to say firstly sixpence for every ton and so in proportion for any less quantity than a ton of all stone of whatever description not exceeding in dimensions in any one piece three cubic feet which shall be prepared, shaped on the said Island especially for pitching, curbing or other street purposes, secondly threepence for every ton and so in proportion for any less quantity than a ton of ore refuse, stone not adapted for building purposes and known as rubble waste or spoils or chips and including stone of an inferior description which may be crushed on the said Island, and thirdly one shilling for every ton and so in proportion for any less Quantity than a ton for all other granite porphyry or other stone whatsoever each to be considered as consisting of twenty hundred weight of one hundred and twelve pounds each and all the said rents and royalties hereby reserved to be paid clear of all presents and future rates and taxes and all other deductions by quarterly payment on the twenty first day of December, the twenty fifth day of March, the twenty fourth day of June and the twenty ninth day of September in every year of the first quarter payment be made on the twenty first day of December next provided always that all royalties which shall become due in any year shall so far as they will extend go toward the payment of the said certain yearly rent of two hundred pounds for the same year but not for any other year each year being considered as ending on the twenty ninth day September to the intent that the total amount payable yearly in respect of the said rent of two hundred pounds and royalties may be two hundred pounds at least and as much more as the royalties in each year shall actually amount to provided always that no royalties shall be payable in respect of any granite porphyry or other stone which shall be used by the said William Columban McKenna. . . in the construction or building of any such breakwater, pier or harbour as he or they, is or are hereinafter authorised to construct or build for his or the private use as hereinbefore is mentioned or in building a church or chapel school-room or reading-room or any messuages or buildings which shall be built by him or them in pursuance of the power in this behalf herein before contained but this proviso shall not apply to any breakwater, harbour building: or improvements for public purposes or which are not hereby expressly authorised to be considered or built by the said William Columban McKenna. . . as aforesaid or to the granite porphyry or other stone and material used in the construction thereof on all which and last mentioned granite porphyry and other stone and material royalties shall be payable at the rate and in manner aforesaid and the said William Columban McKenna doth hereby for himself his heirs, executors and administrators covenant with the said George Williams and Mary Williams and Caroline Helps Morris. . . and also with the said William Hudson Heaven. . . that he the said William Columban McKenna. . . will during the said term pay the said royalty rents of five hundred pounds, and two hundred pounds and all and singular other rents, royalties and reservations hereinafter reserved and made payable as aforesaid at the times and in manner hereinafter appointed for payment of the same respectively without any deduction and also will during the said term bear and pay all rates, taxes, assessments and outgoings whatsoever now or hereafter to become payable whether by the landlord or tenant in respect of the said demised premises or any part thereof and also that he the said William Columban McKenna. . . will from time to time during the said term open quarries of granite porphyry and other stone applicable for building or architectural purposes in or upon the said demised premises and continuously work the same in a proper and workmanlike manner and dress or make marketable all stone raised therefrom and use his and their best endeavours to promote the sale thereof and also that he the said William Columban McKenna, . . . will at all times during the said term when and as any granite porphyry or other stone or market material in respect of which a royalty shall be payable under or by virtue of these presents shall be about to be removed from the said Island fairly and openly, weigh the same and give one day's previous notice at least to the said several persons, parties hereto of the first part. . . and to the said William Hudson Heaven. . . or to their or his agent for the time being at the time or times when such weighing is about to take place by leaving such notice at some place on the said Island to be appointed in writing by the said several persons, parties hereto of the first part ...... and the said William Hudson Heaven. . . to the intent that the said several persons, parties hereto of the first part. . . and the said William Hudson Heaven. . . and their and his agent may be present at and check every such weighing as aforesaid and that he the said William Columban McKenna. . . will keep proper books of account and make true and regular entries therein of all the granite porphyry and other stone and materials gotten or raised by virtue of these presents and of the times when the same shall be removed from the said Island and to whom and how the same shall be sold or disposed of and the weight of the same respective and of all such other matters or things as shall be necessary or expedient to enable said several persons, parties hereto of the first part. . . and the said William Hudson Heaven. . . the better to ascertain the amount of the royalties payable under these presents and will at all reasonable times when required by one weeks previous notice produce at the respective places where the same shall for the time being be usually kept all or any of the such books of account to the said several persons, parties hereto of the first part. . . and to the said William Hudson Heaven. . . and to their or his agents for the time being and permit them and him to take extracts therefrom or copies thereof and will give any explanation which may be required relating thereto and will in all other respects give every possible opportunity and facility to the said several persons, parties hereto of the first part. . . and to the said William Hudson Heaven . . . . and to their and his agent for the time being to ascertain the quantity and weight of all granite porphyry and other stone and material gotten and removed from the said Island by virtue of these presents to the intention that the amount of royalties from time to time payable and becoming payable may be known and for the purpose of effecting this object will concur in any arrangements which may be reasonably proposed and also that he the said William Columban McKenna. . . will at his and their own cost within one calendar month after each of the quarter days on which the rents and the royalties hereby reserved and are made payable deliver to the said several persons, parties hereto of the first part. . . and to the said William Hudson Heaven. . . or leave for them respectively at their respective last known usual places of residence in England or the said Island of Lundy as the case may be or send by post to them respectively addressed to such residences respectively a true account in writing of all the porphyry granite and other stone and materials gotten and carried away during the preceding quarter up to and inclusive of such quarter day and of the quantity and weights thereof and of the times when the same shall have been removed and the persons to whom the same have been sold or consigned and also that he the said William Columban McKenna . . . will at all times during the said term at his and their own costs and charges keep all and singular the quarries which shall for the time being be worked by virtue of these presents and all pits, shafts, levels, embankments, drains, water-courses, buildings, erections, engines, pumps, machinery and plant thereto belonging in good order during the said term at the like costs and charges and shall sufficiently repair and keep repaired and in good order and condition the present farmhouse and all other buildings now existing or which may hereafter be built upon the hereby demised land or any part thereof and all gates, walls, banks, hedges, rails, fences, water- courses, dikes, drains ditches and appurtenances to the said farmhouse, buildings and land or any part thereof belonging except nevertheless the roofs and outer walls of the farmhouse and buildings now existing upon the demised premises and damage happening to the last-mentioned farmhouse and buildings by accident or fit or tempest and also that he the said William Columban McKenna ...... will at the end or sooner determination of the said term hereby granted peaceably and quietly surrender and yield up unto the said several persons, parties hereto of the first part ...... or to the said William Hudson Heaven ditto and singular the said hereby demised premises so well and sufficiently repaired in such good order condition and repair as aforesaid together with all buildings and erections built and erected thereon during the said term and all such fixtures as are or shall be affixed to the freehold of the said premises as between landlord and tenant are usually considered as the property of the landlord but so nevertheless that unless the said term shall be determined by virtue of the power of [   ] hereinafter contained the said William Columban McKenna . . . shall be at liberty to remove for his and their own use all such granite porphyry and other stone and rubble as shall have been properly raised by him or them in pursuance of these presents previously to the termination of the said term the said William Columban McKenna. . . using all reasonable dispatch in removing the same and paying forthwith the full royalties payable in respect thereof and also to remove for his and their own use all engines, machinery and plant erected by the said William Columnar McKenna. . . in or about the said quarries but not any building used in connection with any of the said quarries or any stones or brickwork or timbers or buildings connected with such engines, machinery, plant used for the protection thereof first giving to the said several persons. . . and also to the said William Hudson Heaven. . . the option of purchasing such engines, machinery and plant at a fair valuation to be determined in case of difference by arbitration as hereinafter provided such option to be given by letter addressed and posted to the last known places of abode severally and also that it shall be lawful for the said several persons. . . of the first part and for the said William Hudson Heaven. . . his agents, servants and workmen at any time or times during the said term to enter upon the hereby demised premises or any part thereof for the purpose of inspecting the state and condition thereof and of all faults, decays, or wants of reparation then and there found to give or leave notice in writing upon the hereby demised premises or any part thereof for the said William Columban McKenna. . . and amend the same within three calendar months from the day of the date of such notice within which said time the said William Columban McKenna. . . shall and will repair and amend the same accordingly and that he the said William Columban McKenna. . . will at all times render unto the said several persons. . . of the first part and also unto the said William Hudson Heaven. . . reasonable facility, convenience and assistance for making such inspection as aforesaid and also that he the said William Columban McKenna. . . will not commit any unnecessary damage, spoil or waste in or upon the hereby demised premises or any part thereof in the carrying on the works hereby authorised or in the exercise of any of the powers and privileges conferred upon these persons and will fence round in-a proper manner all such quarries, pits and works as shall be worked or made in pursuance of these presents and also that he the said William Columban McKenna. . . will during the first seven years of the said term expend at least one hundred pounds a year clear of all deductions in draining and wall fencing such of the land hereby demised as shall be used for agricultural purposes and will if required prove such expenditure by the production of all proper vouchers and their satisfactory evidence and will execute all such draining and fencing in a good substantial workmanlike manner provided always that so soon as the sum of seven hundred pound shall have been expended in draining and wall fencing aforesaid within the said seven years the obligation imposed by the said last mentioned covenant shall cease and determine and also that he the said William Columban McKenna. . . will at all times during the said term manage, cultivate and use the arable and pasture lands hereby demised in a good husband-like manner and particularly will not take two white straw crops in any two successive years of the said term from any part of the said lands and will during the last year of the said term cause not less than one equal sixth part of the said arable lands to be properly summer tilled and ploughed and sufficiently harrowed and cultivated and sown with turnips or mangel worzel which are to be twice well hoed and preserved in a clean and proper state and condition for a green crop and will not during the last year of the said term grow any white straw crop on more than a quarter of the said arable lands and will during the last year of the said term call such parts of the said arable lands not exceeding one fourth as aforesaid as shall be devoted to a white straw crop to be properly ploughed and harrowed and sown with barley or oats immediately after turnips or mangel worzel and laid down with a sufficient quantity of good sound clover or other clean artificial grass seeds such as clover or other grass seeds as last aforesaid to be provided by the said William Columban McKenna. . . at the expense of the said several persons, parties of the first part the said William Hudson Heaven. . . but to be sown and harrowed in by the said. . . William Columban McKenna ...... at his and their own cost and the clover and grass rising therefrom to be carefully preserved by the said William Columban McKenna ...... until the end of the said term and also that the said William Columban McKenna .... will spread and consume into muck or dung from cattle in a husbandman-like manner in the farmyard upon the premises hereby demised all the hay, straw, chaff, fodder, turnips, mangel worzel which shall rise from the premises during the said term and shall at reasonable times and in a husbandman-like manner lay and spread such muck or dung upon such parts of the demised lands as shall most need the same, but shall use all the muck or dung to be made previously by the last day of May in the last year of the said term for manuring root crops to be grown in that year and shall leave for the said several persons and parties of the first part. . . and for the said William Hudson Heaven. . . without damaging any allowance or compensation for the same all unused straw grown on the said premises and all the muck, dung and compost which shall be made after the first day of May in the said last year, such muck, dung and compost to be turned up in the yards and premises hereby demised in proper heaps and in a proper manner and also that he the said William Columban McKenna. . . will not if requested not to do by the said several persons. . . or by the said William Hudson Heaven. . . mow any of the lateral grass or meadow or pasturelands for two years successively unless the land intended to be so mown shall have been previously prepared for the second or subsequent mowing by being well and sufficiently manured or watered in a husbandman-like manner and also that he the said William Columban McKenna... will at all times during the said term supply to the said several persons, ... and the said William Hudson Heaven... at cost price all such porphyry granite and other building stone as they or he shall require for the purpose of building any houses, boundary walls or other buildings and erections upon any of the lands hereby reserved to the said several persons... or to William Hudson Heaven... or which they or he are or is by these presents empowered to take or enclose as aforesaid and that the said William Columban McKenna... will not without the previous consent in writing of the said several persons... and the said William Hudson Heaven... build any messuage or other building upon the land hereby demised except such as herein before authorised and also that the said William Columban McKenna... will at any time or times upon the request and at the cost of the said several persons... of the first part and William Hudson Heaven... surrender or assign unto the said several persons... and William Hudson Heaven ... all such parts of the hereby demised premises as shall be enclosed or taken by them respectively in pursuance of any reservations or powers in this behalf hereinbefore contained and also that he the said William Columban McKenna... will at his and their own expense and without payment for such services from time to time at all times during the said term whenever requested so to do convey to the said Island from any vessel or vessels and then convey by hauling or otherwise to the present or any other dwelling house for the time being upon the said Island of the said William Hudson Heaven. . . all such stores, provisions, goods, luggage and effects as shall be brought to the said Island for the said several persons... and for William Hudson Heaven... or their or his servants, friends or visitors and also will at the like expense and without payment for such services from time to time and at all times during the said term whenever requested so to do convey from the dwelling house for the time being on the said Island of the said William Hudson Heaven... to the beach and put on board any vessel or vessels all such goods, luggage and effects belonging to the said several persons... the first part and the said William Hudson Heaven or to their respective servants, friends or visitors as may be required and also that he the said William Columban McKenna ... will from time to time and at all times during the said term convey to land from any vessel or vessels all lime, stone, coal and fuel brought to the said Island for the said several persons... and William Hudson Heaven and stow or stack such limestone on the Quay marked on the plan endorsed on the second skin of the present and such coal in the cellar or cave opening on the said quay and carry and convey such coal and fuel to such dwelling houses as aforesaid being paid in respect of such limestone the sum of four shillings and sixpence for every one hundred bushels and so in proportion for any less quantity and in respect of such coal the sum of eightpence for every ton and so in proportion for any less quantity and in respect of such coal the sum of two shillings for every ton and so in proportion for any less quantity each ton consisting of twenty hundred weights of one hundred a twelve pounds each and that for the purposes aforesaid he the said William Columban McKenna... will at his and their own costs keep or hire all such boats and vessels as may be necessary or expedient with proper crews and tackle for the management of the same and also that he the said William Columban McKenna... will at all times during the said term whenever required so to do give and afford to the said several persons... and

William Hudson Heaven. . . into their and his servants friends and visitors a free passage with such good and proper accommodation as the ship or vessel may conveniently afford on board any ship or vessel belonging to the said William Columban McKenna. . . which shall or may be hired or chartered by him or them and which shall be bound from or to the said Island to or from any part in England and also that he the said William Columban McKenna. . . will whenever required so to do by the said William Hudson Heaven. . . by the said several persons and part. . . subject to the qualification hereinafter mentioned dismiss any person or persons in the employ of the said William Columban McKenna. . . who shall in any way annoy or molest the said William Hudson Heaven. . . or the said several persons . . . or their family, friends or servants or any of them and shall not harbour or give lodgings to or in any way assist or countenance such person or persons and will dismiss such person or persons as aforesaid when requested so to do by the said William Hudson Heaven. . . without requiring any cause to be assigned for such dismissal, but that by any other case the said William Columban McKenna....will not be bound to dismiss such person or persons as aforesaid without a reasonable cause for such dismissal being assigned and proved and also that he the said William Columban McKenna. . . will at all time: during the said term furnish and deliver on the said Island to the said several persons. . . and William Hudson Heaven. . . and his family servants and friends all such milk butter and other produce of the farm as they or he shall require at the farm, average market price for articles of the like nature and quality in the town of BIDEFORD in the County of Devon such price to be determined in case of difference by the Mayor of BIDEFORD for the time being and that he the said William Columban McKenna . . . . will not during the said term hunt, hawk, shoot or sport or give permission to any person or persons to hunt, hawk, shoot or sport in or upon the said Island or any part thereof except for the purpose of killing rabbits other than by shooting on any part of the demised premises situate to the north of a line to be drawn from the north side of the northward most valley of Gannets Combe on the east straight across the Island to the west without the consent in 'writing of the said several persons. . . and William Hudson Heaven. . . for that purpose on each occasion previously obtained and that he the said William Columban McKenna. . . will warn off all persons who during the said term shall hunt, hawk, shoot or sport upon the said Island without such consent as aforesaid and will give to the several persons, parties hereto of the first part. . . and William Hudson Heaven leave for them respectively at their respective last known usual places of residence in England or the said Island of Lundy as the case may be or sent by post to them respectively at such residences respectively immediate notice of the fact of any person, hunting, hawking, shooting or sporting upon the said Island without such consent as aforesaid and that it shall be lawful for the said several persons. . . and William Hudson Heaven. . . in case any person or persons shall during the said term hunt, hawk, shoot or sport on the said premises. . . to bring any action or suit and prosecute the same at law or otherwise proceed against such persons in the name or names of the said William Columban McKenna. . . or any of them and that the said William Columban McKenna. . . will not release or discharge any such action suit or proceedings without the consent in writing of the said several persons. . . and William Hudson Heaven but the said William Columban McKenna. . . shall be indemnified by the said William Hudson Heaven. . . and against the cost thereof provided always that all notices and accounts which under the foregoing covenants the said William Columban McKenna. . . is and are required to give to the said several persons. . . and William Hudson Heaven . . . to leave at or send to their respective residences shall by writing inform the said William Columban McKenna. . . to be considered as properly given, left or sent if given, left or sent to or at the residence or respective residences of the said William Hudson Heaven. . . provided always and it is hereby agreed and declared that if the rents and royalties hereinbefore reserved or any part thereof respectively shall be unpaid for three calendar months next after any of the days hereinbefore appointed for the payment thereof wherever the same shall have been legally demanded or not or if breach shall be made in any of the covenants. . . conditions or agreements in these presents contained and on the part of the said William Columban McKenna. . . to be observed or performed then and in any of such cases it shall be lawful for the said several persons. . . in the name of the whole to render and the same premises to have again as in their former state and from thereafter the said term hereby granted shall absolutely cease and determine and be the said George Williams so far only as relates to the acts and deeds of himself and the said Mary Williams his wife doth hereby for himself. . . and she the said Caroline Helps Morris so far as relates to her own acts and deeds alone doth hereby for herself, for. . . covenant with the said William Columban McKenna. . . that it shall be lawful for the said William Columban McKenna. . . paying the rents and royalties hereby reserved and performing and observing all and every the covenants and conditions in these presents contained and which on his or their part or parts ought to be performed and observed peaceably to hold and enjoy the hereby demised premises during the term hereby granted without any lawful interaction or disturbance by the said George Williams, Mary Williams, Caroline Helps Morris or any of them and the said William Hudson Heaven doth hereby for himself. . . covenant with the said William Columban McKenna. . . that he the said William Hudson Heaven. . . will not during the said term carry away or knowingly permit to be carried away from the said Island any granite porphyry or other building stone obtained from any parts of the said Island not comprised in these presents and also that he the said William Hudson Heaven. . . will from time to time and at all times during the said term at his and their own cost unless repair shall have been rendered necessary thereto by any neglect on the part of the said William Columban McKenna. . . repair and keep in good order and condition buildings now existing upon the land hereby demised but not those of any other house or buildings the said William Columban McKenna. . . to the said William Hudson Heaven. . . reasonable notice in writing of any defects or wants of reparation in such rooms or outer walls as aforesaid and that if the said farmhouse or other buildings now existing on the hereby demised land or any of them shall at any time or times during the said term be destroyed or damaged by accidental fire and not through the agency of any incendiary or by tempest then and in every such case that he the said William Hudson Heaven. . . will at his and their own cost when necessary and upon every reasonable request and timely notice in writing given to him or them by the said William Columban McKenna. . . furnish to the said William Columban McKenna. . . at some convenient place on the northern coast or Devonshire to be selected by the said William Hudson Heaven. . . sufficient rough timber, tiles, lime and iron except gate irons, for repairing the farmhouse and buildings now existing upon the hereby demised premises and also the now existing gates, posts, stiles and fences thereupon but not any other houses, buildings, gates, posts, stiles and fences all such timber, tiles, lime and iron as aforesaid... [Page 14 missing.] ..... and the said William Hudson Heaven that if the said William Columban McKenna shall be desirous of taking a new Lease of the hereby demised premises after the expiration of the term hereby granted and shall so indicate six calendar months before the expiration thereof signifying such desire by notice in writing delivered to the said William Hudson Heaven... at their usual or last known place of residence on the said Island of Lundy or England... in the present contained and on the part of the said William Columban McKenna... to be observed and performed and kept in such cases the said William Hudson Heaven and all other necessary parties will at or before the expiration of the said time hereby granted at cost of the said William Columban McKenna... execute him or them a fresh Lease of the hereby demised premises for a similar term of fourteen years six months from the expiration of the term hereby granted at and under a yearly rent of six hundred pounds for the service of the said premises and under a further yearly rent of two hundred pounds and to be payable whether any granite or porphyry or other stone shall be gotten or not and under the like royalty in addition to the said service rent and the said yearly rent of two hundred pounds and faith and subject to the like covenants, provisos and grievance as are hereto contained except the proviso for the first seven years of the term to be granted thereby but including this present covenant for renewal, being the intention of the parties hereto that the said Lease and the term hereby granted shall be from time to time renewable and perpetuity, but so nevertheless that in every renewed Lease except the first renewed Lease of which the service rent to be six hundred pounds as aforesaid the rent reserved in respect of the services the demised premises shall be such a rent at the time of granting such Lease shall by fact improved, a fair improved rent for the demised land and the houses and improvements then upon the same regarded as agricultural property and without taking into consideration any of the quarries worked on the premises or the buildings or machinery erected for the purposes of working the same such rent in case of dispute be determined by other arbitration in manner heretofore provided but in no case to be less than six hundred pounds a year, and provided always that on every occasion of a renewal of a party or parties to whom the same shall be granted do and shall at his or their own expense execute a counterpart of the new Lease so to be granted and it is hereby agreed by and between all parties hereto that when and so soon as any such new Lease shall be granted the covenants and provisions of the preceeding Lease especially relating to the farming and the cultivation of the premises during the last year of the term thereby granted or to the giving up of the same premises shall be annulled and determined and this thereby also agreed and declared between and by the said William Columban McKenna... and the said William Hudson Heaven that the said William Columban McKenna... shall on the twenty ninth day of September next take at a valuation and then pay to the said William Hudson Heaven... for such crops, livestock and farming and agricultural implements as shall on the twenty fifth day of September next be in or about the hereby demised premises, and as such furniture and household effects as shall then be in or about the farmhouse or any other... messuages hereby demised shall such valuation to be determined in case of dispute by arbitration as hereinafter provided, provided always and it is hereby agreed and declared that it shall be lawful for the said William Columban McKenna... if he or they shall think it fit so to do to enter upon any part of the hereby demised land which lies to the north of the wall marked Quarter Wall on the plan endorsed on

ADDENDUM

Since going to Press the missing page 14 of the Heaven/McKenna lease has come to light.

. . .be by the said William Columban McKenna his executors etc. at his or their own expense bought from the coast of Devonshire as aforesaid and landed on the Island of Lundy and hauled from the landing place to the place or places where the same shall be required to be used and also that he the said William Hudson Heaven etc. will at the end of the said term of the present Lease shall not be renewed in pursuance of the provision in this behalf hereinafter contained and shall not be determined in pursuance of the proviso for re-entry hereinbefore contained take at a valuation the dead farming stock and serviceable implements of husbandry belonging to the said William Columban McKenna his executors etc. then used upon the hereby demised premises and also such crops of potatoes, turnips, mangel wurzels as shall have been properly sown and cultivated according to the stipulations herein contained and shall then in the ground and also such of the then last years hay as shall be left on the said premises, such hay to be valued as to be consumed on the premises and shall also allow or pay to the said William Columban McKenna, his executors etc. for all such clover or grass seeds as shall have been sown by him or them in accordance with these presence with the summer corn in the last year of the said term and the value of the said farming stock implements, crops and hay and the sum to be paid for such clover and grass seeds as last aforesaid to be determined in case of dispute by arbitration in manner hereinafter provided but so nevertheless that under the present covenant the said William Hudson Heaven etc. shall not be obliged to take a greater quantity of dead farming stock and implements of husbandry and shall be reasonably sufficient for the cultivation of proper farming of such parts of the hereby demised premises as shall not at the end of the said term be devoted to agricultural purposes, and also that it shall be lawful for the said William Columban McKenna etc. to pay the said yearly rents and royalties hereby reserved and observing and performing all the covenants, conditions and agreements in these presence contained and on his and their part to be observed and performed peaceably to hold and enjoy all and singular the hereby demised premises during the said term hereby granted without any lawful interaction or disturbance by the said William Hudson Heaven or his heirs etc. or acquitted of the claiming or to claim through under or in trust for him, them or any of them provided always and it is hereby agreed and declared between and by the parties hereto that if the said William Columban McKenna, etc. shall be desirous to determine the present demise at the end of the first seven years of the term of fourteen years hereby granted and shall deliver to the said several persons, parties hereto of the first part etc. and the said William Hudson Heaven etc. or shall leave at their respective usual or last known place of abode etc. as the case maybe twelve calendar months previous notice in writing such his or their desires and shall pay all arrears of rents and royalties and perform all and every the covenants herein contained and on his or their part to be observed and performed then and in such ease immediately after the expiration of such for seven years of the said term this present Lease and the term hereby granted shall cease and determine provided always and it is hereby agreed and declared between and by the said William Columban McKenna. . .

the second skin of these presents before the twenty ninth day of September one thousand eight hundred and sixty three for the purpose of commencing quarrying operations or any buildings connected therewith but not for any other purpose the said William Columban McKenna. . . in such cases paying in respect of a period between such entry on the land and the commencement of the present Lease a proportional part of the said yearly rent of two hundred pounds and all such royalties as would have been payable under these presents for such period if the present Lease had taken effect in interest from the time of such entry as aforesaid and also making reasonable compensation for any injury which he or they may occasion to the farm, farming stock or crops and such compensation to be determined in case of which. . . [wanting]. . . dispute by arbitration as hereinafter provided, and it is hereby agreed and declared between and by the parties hereto that if any difference or dispute which is not hereby expressly directed to be determined by the Mayor of BIDEFORD at the time being shall arise between the said William Columban McKenna. . . and the said several persons and William Hudson Heaven, or between any of the persons aforesaid touching the construction of these presents or anything herein contained or any valuation, compensation or price to be made given, paid or allowed under these presents or touching any other matter or thing arising out of these presents or having any valuation to the premises, then and in every such case such a difference or dispute shall be referred to the arbitration of three indifferent persons one to be chosen by each of the differing or disputing parties within one calendar month after either of them shall have made to the other a requisition to the effect, and the third by the two persons first chosen within one calendar month after either of them shall have been themselves chosen and if either of the differing or disputing parties shall in writing require the other of the said parties to refer the dispute or difference to arbitration have to name an arbitrator and if the party to whom such requisition is made shall for one calendar month after such a requisition refuse or neglect to comply therewith or shall name a person who shall neglect or refuse to act as arbitrator, then it shall be lawful for the person chosen on behalf of the party making such requisition by writing under his hand to appoint some person to act as arbitrator on behalf of the other party and such two persons shall name a further arbitrator as aforesaid and that the said arbitrators or any two of them shall determine an award concerning the matters and things referred to them for arbitration and if they shall see fit so to do require the aid and take the opinion of any accountant, council or other person and adopt such other measures as shall appear to them expedient and that the parties so differing or disputing as aforesaid and all persons claiming through them respectively shall in all things. . . obey, abide by, observe and to form the award of the aforesaid arbitrators or of any two of them so as the award of the said arbitrators or as such two of them as shall so concur be made in writing under their hands and be ready to be delivered to the said parties respectively or to such of them as shall desire the same within three calendar months next after the nomination of the arbitrator and that the said parties so differing or disputing as aforesaid and all persons claiming through them respectively shall if required by the said arbitrators or any two of them attend personally and submit to be examined relative to the matters or things referred to arbitration and produce to and deposit with said arbitrators or any two of them all deeds, letters, papers, writings and evidences relative thereto and do all other things which the said arbitrators or any two of them shall require and the said parties respectively and all persons claiming through them respectively if examined and all other witnesses shall if thought proper by such arbitrators be examined upon oath or upon information in cases where information is allowed by law instead of oath and that the expenses of the arbitration including compensation to be made by the arbitrator for their trouble and fees and compensation to be made to any accountant, council or other persons who may be called on as aforesaid shall be in the discretion of the said arbitrators or any two of them who shall direct by whom and to whom and in what manner the same shall be paid and who shall be at liberty if they see fit to direct that all or any of such cost and expenses shall be reckoned as between the termee and client or as between parties and party or otherwise and any reference to arbitration under any by virtue of these presents may be made a rule of any of her Majesty's Courts at Westminster according to the statute in that case and made and provided if such court shall be so pleased and either party shall be at liberty to reply to any of the said courts to act on and instruct council to consent thereto for the other party and wherein by any indenture dated the twentyfirst day of February one thousand eight hundred and forty four and made between the said William Hudson Heaven on the one part and the said Mary Williams then Mary Lowsley and the laid Caroline Helps Norris of the other part the said Island and premises with the appurtenances where to the said Mary Williams and Caroline Helps Morris and their heirs upon trust to secure the repayment of the principle and interest money therein mentioned and in the said indenture is contained a power authorising the said Mary Williams and the said Caroline Helps Morris and their heirs to sell the said Island and hereditaments to secure the repayment of the said principle and interest money and in the said indent it is provided that the said power and estate should not be executed unless and until any notice in writing should have been previously given to the said William Hudson Heaven. . . requiring him or them to pay off the monies which for the time being should be due on the security of the said indenture or such a notice should have been left at his or their usual or last known place of residence or abode in England or Wales and default should have been made in payment of such monies or some part thereof for the space of six calendar months to be computed from the time of giving or leaving such notice or unless the interest should be in arrears as therein mentioned, now this indenture further witnesseth that each of them the said George William and Caroline Helps Morris for himself and herself and his and her . . . doth hereby covenant the said William Columban McKenna. . . that the said power of sale shall not be executed unless and until such a notice as is required to be given as aforesaid shall be given to the said William Columban McKenna. . . or that for him or them at his or their last known place of abode in England and default shall be made in payment of such monies or such part thereof for the space of six calendar months to the intent that unless the said William Hudson Heaven his heirs or assigns shall pay or cause to be paid the said principle monies and interest one month at least before the expiration of the said notice the said William Columban McKenna. . . may pay off the money due upon such mortgage and any further charge on the said premises already effected and take a transfer of the securities for the same and notice of this covenant shall be endorsed on the said indenture of mortgage and witness thereof the said parties to these presents have hereunder unto set their hands and sealed the day and year first before written.

APPENDIX III

W.H. Heaven's correspondence regarding the marketing of Lundy granite.

Thomas Helps to W.H. Heaven

London 27 October 1838

'My Dear Sir,
Immediately on receipt of your letter making an offer to the Committee for the Management of the Building of the Royal Exchange of sufficient granite from the Island of Lundy, I caused the offer to be laid before the Committee. I have called at the Town Clerk's office to enquire what progress has been made. The reply was the gentleman had had several meetings on the subject of your liberal offer but as yet no decision had been come to – in a few days no doubt we shall get an answer. Please to present my kind regards to Mrs Heaven and believe me my dear Sir

Yours Truly
Tho. Helps
Advanced to Walton House, Bristol. . . . .'

*

Thomas Spargo to W.H. Heaven

2 Jan 1839

Hon. Sir, I beg leave to inform you that by the order of Mr. W.R. Broad of Falmouth I left Penryn Sept. 10th 1838 for the purpose of inspecting into the nature and quality of the Moorstone Granite that I might find on Lundy Island. . . and to make any other observation that I might deem advisable relative to the shipment thereof. I have to observe that I arrived on the Island on Sept. 12th following, and next morning in company with, Mr. Hope perceeded [sic] to different parts of the Island for the purpose stated above and in answer have to acquaint you that I found some very excellent granite Stone generally, but especially on the eastern side of the Island. I found very good stone for Building Peair, [sic], Pier Heads, Quays or Docks, and which might be brought to the place of shipping at a trifling expense and in consequence of such a numerous quantity of Granite Stone on the Island, I think it would be advisable and advantageous to your Honor to cause a Place or kind of Quay to be erected for the purpose of vessels taking in their cargoes. There is a good quality of Granite Stone on the Western Side of the Light House but that will attend [sic] to great expense to come at being bound with other stone of bad Quality.

I remain, Hon. Sir
Your M: Ob.t Servant
Thomas Spargo
I have received of Mr. W.R. Broad towards my time and expenses the sum of £5. 0s. 0d which my Demand is now from the Mr. W.R. Broad three pounds more.
January 2nd 1839

*

W. R. Broad to W. H. Heaven

Falmouth, 3rd January 1839

My dear Sir,
By some unaccountable means I did not get your letter dated 15th Decr until the 21st following – however I lost no time in communicating your wishes to Spargo who called at our office yesterday and left the annexed which I hope will answer your purpose – if not, and you wish his ideas in any other form on your signifying the same to me I will get it done.

I gave him £5 to go to Lundy and it appears his demand is £3 more – which includes every expense of going and returning – he told me the other day that he was confident there is capital Granite on the Island and could you once introduce it in London or any place where any Public Works are carrying on it would be an excellent thing for you. I would if I had been you make a great effort to supply the Gresham Committee for the Exchange – the benefit of such a thing would be incalculable. In the hope you may succeed in this and with our united regards to Mrs. Heaven and your flock.

I remain, My dear Sir
Yours very faithfully
W. R. Broad   [Addressed to W. H. Heaven Esq. Walton House, Nr Bristol.]

*

Adam Murray to W. H. Heaven

3rd June 1839

47 Parliament Street
W. H. Heaven Esq.
Sir,
I have now had an interview with my East India friend who has suddenly altered his mind and declines making an offer for Lundy Island, which I am sorry for. He requests me to make an apology to you for the trouble he has put you to.
I have the honour to be
Sir, respectfully
You obedient servant
Adam Murray   [Addressed to Walton Castle, Bristol]

On the reverse:

Dear Ashfield,
On the other side you may see the result of the Murray affair.
For sprains etc:
2 new laid eggs $1/2$ pint verjuice – 2oz camphorated oil
2 T [easpoons] Turps - mix well, and rub in twice a day.
All well,
Yours as ever
W. H. Heaven
[Addressed to A. C. Hope Esq. C. G. Heaven, Solicitor, Bristol]

*

John D. Heesewell to W. H. Heaven

Plymouth 13 July 1841

My dear Sir,
In accordance with my promise I have made enquiries relative to the working of Granite and as to that sort that will be most saleable…permit me to express my regret at not being able to accompany you to the island.
I will just here say I have seen a captain of a vessel who has been at anchor in Lundy roads several times he tells me the anchorage is safe with any wind from SSW round by West to NNW and is of the opinion that a single mooring might be laid down for vessels when loading to ride at so that if the wind should go suddenly round to the Eastward it might slip and run either for Milford – Barnstaple and if northerly to Ilfracombe but this would be an after consideration when you find from experience that the expense would be worth going into.
The quarrying of the stone is………[there follows a general account of the qualities of granite and the prices paid for various grades, colours, qualities etc. and the cost of tools necessary and the particular requirements of some markets]
One load of curb stones was sent from Plymouth to Bristol – might there be a good market found there for the Lundy Island stone – if only for street paving – curbs, door steps…[describes the necessity of care to be taken in selecting stone to be worked before expending money on labour to work it]
It would be necessary to have a man a thorough judge of stone, and how it lays in the quarries to say whether it would be worth working – I find that most of the granite works in England and Scotland are working by [illegible] when they hear of a good stone or quarry being worked generally strive to get it in their own hands which was lately tried at Penryn without success.

Yours very truly
John D. Heeswell

*

The Revd H. G. Heaven to H. Benthall

Lundy Island June 30th 1870

To H. Benthall
Dear Sir,
Mr Wilkins has been to me with reference to shipping away another cargo of stone, but I have told him I cannot in any way consent, in my father's absence, to allow any more to leave the Island till the money for the last cargo is remitted to the Island, or its equivalent in farming stock, seeds or other goods for Island use. It may be that without formal seizure we might find a difficulty, in a legal point of view merely, in absolutely preventing the removal of the stone; but I should certainly refuse to allow any assistance, as hitherto, being given by our men in the shipping of the stone, and if the attempt be made shall do all I can to get my Father to immediately make the necessary formal and legal seizure. In this I think he would be quite justified after the undertaking given by you to allow all the proceeds of the stone removed to be remitted to the island. It is not the mere idleness of the quarries that is in question alone, but the ruinous deterioration of the estate as a Farm which is going on at the same time for want of stocking and

proper cropping and labour. The arable lands are now covered with a crop of weeds going to seed, sufficient to cause the expenditure of hundreds in labour for the eradication of them in future years. I am told that McKenna (E. McKenna) receives payments every fortnight for the stone he delivers on orders. There can be no reason than why the money or its equivalent according to our agreement should not be remitted when the vessel comes for a fresh cargo from time to time; and then we would gladly facilitate the departure of the stone, believing it to be as much to our advantage as to yours that the stone should get into the market. But I cannot see that it is at all to our advantage that everything should go off the Island while not a pennyworth returns to it, and all on it is going to ruin. My father is in Bristol now and if you wish to communicate with him you had better write through his solicitors.

In much haste,
Yours faithfully.
H.G. Heaven

*

The Revd H. G. Heaven to Henry Benthall

Lundy Island
July 8th 1870

To H. Benthall.

Dear Sir,
I beg to acknowledge receipt of your letter of the 5th inst. I have shown it to my Father (who has returned to the Island) and he agrees with me, that it would be undesirable to allow another cargo of stone to be taken away before the remittance to Lundy of the amount due for the last. Neither my Father nor myself doubt in the least your intention of fulfilling the agreement you entered into when here but it seems to us useless to send another cargo from the island, if that already sent is not sold, and if sold undesirable until the price of it is sent here. As to any legal proceedings my Father may take or has taken he only acts under the special direction of his solicitors but we regret, that what they deem necessary should cause you any inconvenience.

I remain, dear Sir,
Yours faithfully, H. G. Heaven

*

The Revd H. G. Heaven to H Benthall: July 14th 1870

Lundy Island,
July 14th 1870

To H. Benthall.

Dear Sir,
Mr Wilkins has handed me yours of the 12th and I am glad to find that we seem to be agreed in the interpretation of our compact.

I suppose Mr Wilkins will hardly require the full value at once of a cargo in store or goods, so I hope Mr McKenna (E. McKenna) will be instructed to bring a moiety of the value of it in cash, or at any rate a large proportion of it. We want labour badly in the Island both for saving the harvest and shipping the stone, but wages must be paid for labour and therefore cash <u>must</u> form part of the proceeds sent over. I am glad you have stated that the goods are to be invoiced, and allow me to suggest that a properly drawn up accounting of the value of the stone sold be sent with the invoice of goods and cash sent. There can arise no unpleasantness between the various parties, as to the actual equality in value between the goods and cash sent, and the cargo of stone previously removed. You know the general feeling on the Island regarding the trustworthiness of your agent (Wilkins) on the other side, and I am sure what I suggest will alone obviate squabbles in the matter.

In much haste,
Yours faithfully,
H. G. Heaven

*

APPENDIX IV

A Miscellany of Extracts & Cuttings

'St James (Parkham, North Devon) has a fine late-Norman south doorway and font. The rest of the church is 15th-century with early 16th- century aisles - the north one was built by the Risdons of Bableigh, and the south by the Giffards of Halsbury. The arcades are of Lundy granite; brought down from the top of Lundy island, the stone underwent a fifteen mile passage by sea before the masons could use it.'

Dunning M. 2001

*

February 1864
£5,005 paid for deposit in the name of a director of the National Bank in the Weald and Kent Railway as 'normal investment of capital.'
Purchase of the *Vanderbyl*, appointment of James Press as captain.

National Archives

*

North Devon Journal, 31 March 1864
County Magistrates Petty Sessions, Sat. 21st inst. Ilfracombe.

Suicide at Lundy Island

'On Tuesday morning a man was brought from Lundy Island, who in the early part of that day had committed suicide. . . The deceased, who was a Scotchman called George Courige, apparently about 40 years of age, was engaged a few months ago as clerk by the Company who are digging granite at Lundy Island. He appeared to be a very respectable, intelligent man, but of a melancholy, reserved disposition. He was known to have been about 11 years in India, and while there to have suffered from sun-stroke, and once, during his stay at Lundy, symptoms of mental deficiency were exhibited. . . On Sunday night deceased slept in the same room with another person, Mr Patrick Delley, surveyor. This gentleman rose about six o'clock, leaving his companion asleep. . . about 8 o'clock Mr Delley again returned to his room and, on beginning to ascend the stairs, was startled to see deceased dangling by a slight cord to the banister. . . the unfortunate man was cut down, but life was found to be quite extinct. Measures were taken without delay to convey the body to Ilfracombe. . . the jury returned a verdict that the deceased committed suicide whilst labouring under temporary insanity. Deceased is said to have been a single man, very respectably connected.'

*

'A tender from the Lundy Granite Company was laid before the Committee. . . offering to supply the Lighthouse on the Island with coal at 29s 6d per ton, and the Fog Signal Establishment at 33s per ton, which was excepted.'
[The higher price for the Fog Station reflects the steep access to the cottages, where a cart could not be used.]

Trinity House Archive

*

September 1864
A steamship, the *Vanderbyl*, shipped at Barnstaple cattle and other supplies for the use of employees of the Lundy Island Granite Co.

North Devon Record Office, D. O. 040

*

Exeter Flying Post, 29 November 1865
Lundy Island is manifesting its entire independence. The other day an attempt was made to rate the owner of the granite company to the police rate; but he resented the interference by forbidding the police to land upon the island. The immunity which the island has enjoyed by the absence of the officers of justice has made it a refuge for those who felt the mainland too hot for them. It is not surprising, therefore, that the prohibition against the police has been extended to county court officers and the inhabitants revel in fancied security. County Court summonses to persons at Lundy have been unanswered, and Mr. Sarjeant Petersdorff, the judge, has indicated his intention of bringing the matter under the notice of the Court of Queen's Bench.

*

'I first went to Lundy in 1867. . . The Granite Company had about a hundred men there to work on the island and the stores was kept open to sell beer every day and the pilots from Bristol would come up there very often after the beer till they got drunk. . . We used to come up to Lundy in the summer time at April month and go home to another fishery in the winter. . .'
George Thomas, fisherman

Harman archive

*

September 1867
At Barnstaple County Court before His Honour Judge Sarjeant Petersdorff, the High Bailiff, stated that he had been unable to serve the summons on a defendant on Lundy Island. The officer went to a steamer which traded with the island and the captain positively refused to allow him to sail in her stating that he had received orders from the company not to allow a bailiff to set foot upon the Island. His Honour said there was clearly a conspiracy amongst the inhabitants of the Island to defeat the ends of justice. He had communicated with the Solicitor to the Treasury and he was collecting evidence on the matter. The hearing of the case was postponed *sine die*.   North Devon Record Office, D.O. 040, p. 117, col. 2.

January 1868
The steamer *East Anglian* was wrecked off Lundy, the crew being saved.
North Devon Record Office, D.O. 040, p.124, col. 3.

*

North Devon Journal Herald, 3rd September 1868
John Brogden & Sons announced that the screw steamer, *Ogmore*, would run weekly from Porthcawl Dock to Fremington Quay with best house coal.

*

April 1871
'Northover, Dicky Walters and Dennis the Blacksmith being out of the Company's service, they were taken on by Grandfather [W.H. Heaven].
July 1871
'. . . two Frenchmen came up in the evening, whom the islanders supposed to be smugglers seeking Mr Wilkins as a customer, who had already left the island.'

Harman archive

*

12th August 1869
'Lundy Granite Company – An application was made on Thursday to the Chief Clerk, Rolls Chambers, for a settlement of a claim between Lundy Granite Company and the Somerset & Dorset Railway Company. Mr. R Miller appeared for the Granite Company and Messrs. Toogood for the Railway Company. The dispute originally was as to the price that should be paid for a piece of land needed by the Granite Company after a lease and the sum of £75 was ultimately agreed upon. The parties now asked the Chief Clerk to settle a weekly sum to be paid by the Granite Company during their occupation of the land from the 10th July, the time when they should have removed the stone upon it. The Chief Clerk split the difference between the sum mentioned by the parties and made an order of 6s per week.'

National Archives

*

GRANITE COMPANY GRAVES ON LUNDY

1. Erected by Thomas Spearman in memory of his father, WILLIAM SPEARMAN who died Dec 22nd. Aged 52 years.
2. In memory JAMES YOUNG. Land Surveyor and Valuator of Perth who died here 5th Feb 1865. Aged 63 years.
[James Young, retired, was visiting his daughter, and her husband, who had come to Lundy to manage the island on behalf of the granite company].
3. Erected by John KYLE of Glasgow in memory of ALEXANDER his brother, who died 6th September 1864 aged 17 years. ALEXANDER his son, who died 30th March 1865, aged 14 months.

*

24 September 1869
The liquidator made an application to the court '...to prosecute an action in Her Majesty's Court of Exchequer of Pleas. . . against George Thomas of Tenby. . . for the payment of a promissory note for £99.1.7 given. . . for granite supplied to him. . . by the company at his request.' [His cheque had been dishonoured.]

National Archives

*

EXCERPT FROM THE HEAVEN FAMILY LUNDY LOG

Just above [the quarries] were two buildings known as the Hospital and the Surgery, and close by was a long row of cottages and a well. . . and another row by the Quarter Wall were pulled down for repairs of masonry and also to build the church [1897]. Three better class cottages on E. Side, south of the Wm Hird's Quarry, were occupied by the Clerk of the Works in North Cottage; Dr Linacre and his successor, Dr Snow, on South Cottage and the manager of the Quarries, Mr Kyle, in Middle Cottage. . . they were void from 1868 to 1872.

The Company built the Store and the adjoining cottage. . . they employed a Baker, who lived over the Store – the bakery was in that part of the Store nearest the Bakehouse Field [present Tent Field]. In the cottage in the farm garden Jones the shoemaker was domiciled. Where the Rickyard now is were three or four dormitories. . . wooden buildings covered with felt tarred black, and in derision called Golden Square – in winter, occasionally, dances took place here. Between Barton Cottages and the Barn was a corrugated iron structure used for church purposes, as a school, Magic Lantern exhibitions, and parish Sewing Meetings…the Company was building the 'Big House' extension to the old farm as a Boarding House. Among the Company's employees were many Irish and Scotch men – men from Aberdeen – chiefly of the latter…

*

Near the Quarter Wall Cottages was a smithy.

Harman archive

*

Extract from *Devon* by W.G. Hoskins – 1954:
(included by kind permission of the copyright holder)

ALWINGTON church (St. Andrew) stands beside an ancient, grey barton. It is almost entirely 15th century with a handsome tapered tower; the S. aisle and porch were rebuilt in the 17th century. The nave arcade is of Lundy granite. The Portledge pew, at the E. end of the S. aisle, is made up of pieces from the Elizabethan minstrels' gallery at Portledge, and the reredos from old bench-ends taken out of Parkham church in 1806. The pulpit is made up largely from bench-ends in Alwington church itself; one of the remaining bench-ends is dated 1580. The mural monuments of the Coffins of Portledge are worth attention, especially that to Richard Coffin (1617) and Elizabeth his wife (1651) and their fifteen children.

*

From John Norton, F.R.I.B.A., architect of St Helen's Church on Lundy

2 February, 1897

Dear Sirs,

You asked me to express my opinion of Lundy granite, as having just used it in the constitution of the Church of St Helen's, on the island; I am well qualified to give an opinion.

Upon my first visit to the island the owner took me to see the disused quarries, three of which remain on the eastern cliffs, which fairly astonished me – one showing a clean perpendicular height of 100 feet and another of 80 feet – enormous blocks lay on the plateau formed at the base of the quarries; from these blocks (left by former workings) I directed my contractors to work, for facing the walls of the church and tower, and it gives me pleasure to assure you no finished masonry ever gave me such complete satisfaction.

As to the durability of the stone there can be no doubt, as proved by a visit to the old lighthouses, exposed as they are to the Atlantic gales. . [they] as if worked yesterday. I am thus fully persuaded that the walls of the church will last as long as the Island, and that I am fully justified in recommending the use of Lundy granite for dock and other cognate works, as well as for ordinary architectural purposes.

The important information you are collecting as to costs of quarrying and working the stone and of water conveyance to various ports appears to show that no other source of supply can compare with Lundy, and I foresee a great demand for the granite as soon as you can get to work on the new quarries you contemplate opening near the sea level, to say nothing of the existing source of supply from the three upper quarries already opened.

Congratulating you upon procuring such a valuable concession,

I am, Dear Sir, yours faithfully. . .

*

From Mr. Harry Hems, of Ecclesiastical Art Works, Exeter
5 February 1897
'. . .For high-class work we prefer Lundy granite to any other we know.'

Harman archive

*

September 1899 (source as yet unidentified)

'We are informed that a strong syndicate in conjunction with West of England and South Wales capitalists, are about to open up the valuable granite quarries on Lundy Island. Last week a party of representatives of these, with a leading Westminster engineer, were taking soundings and arranging for a comprehensive serial cable tramway system to load the granite into steam crafts that will convey it to Devon, South Wales and other outports. The steam vessels will also, it is hoped, in the future be a means of more frequent communications with the island for visitors. The granite was worked to some extent many years ago, and several of our greatest constructive works, such as the Thames Embankment, are stated to have been principally built from the stone. With modern methods and better facilities for shipment, the re-opening of the quarries seems capable of being made the starting point of an important industry.'

*

Western Morning News, 2nd June 1922

Lundy Island and S. Endellion

Sir,

I read with interest your article on Lundy Island. When I came to the parish I was informed that the tower of S. Endellion came from 'the Kingdom of Heaven.' I was greatly puzzled as to the meaning of this. I soon discovered that the granite for the tower was quarried at Lundy Island, which belonged to a family called Heaven, and the island was their kingdom. . .

F.P. LUIGI JOSA

S. Endellion Rectory, Port Isaac.

*

APPENDIX V

MAY 1871
INVENTORY OF DEFICIENCIES IN THE ASSETS ON LUNDY THAT WERE TAKEN OVER BY H. BENTHALL 24 JUNE 1869

Edward McKenna and Charles John Schneider, 5-6 May 1871.
[McKenna had also taken the inventory on 24 June 1869]

INCLINE	Chain and gear wagons displaced
SMITHS POINT QUARRY	1 Chain to 10 ton crane missing
MIDDLE QUARRY	1 Sling chain missing
HOWARDS QUARRY	Crab winches displaced... 1.5 ton crab winch (broken).
Missing:	
	60 ft three-quarter inch chain, 2 sheet blocks and 1 quarry screw jack, Work shed (half blown down) – Workman's call bell missing.
QUARRY TOOLS MISSING	11 x 2½in bore quarry jumpers, 6 navvy shovels, 3 picks, 1 screw cramp
SMITHY Missing	1 dozen old files, 2 screw dies (no taps), 23 jumpers, 20 x 2½ inch borers, 6 cast steel borers, 37 pieces half inch iron, 2 bundles nail rods, 1 bar hose shoe iron, 1½ square bolt iron, 8 bars blister steel, and 12 bars flat shear steel.
SOUTH END VILLA	Upstairs, missing: 3 mattresses, 2 pillows and 1 flock tic
Kitchen, missing:	fire irons and galvanised buckets
Parlor:	deal table found broken, fender broken
Sleeping apartment downstairs, missing:	towel horse mattress flock, tic bolster.
Wash House, missing:	beer [?] zinc bucket
Yard, missing:	portable poultry house
MIDDLE VILLA Parlor:	carpet worn out and valueless
No 2, missing:	looking glass, mattress, 6 blankets, 1 counterpane, 4 sheets, 2 table covers, jug, basin and chamber.
No 3, missing:	mattress, 2 pillows
No 4, missing:	3 trays, salt box, 2 irons, 2 large dishes.
No 5, missing:	mattress, feather, bolster, 2 flock ditto, 1 rug, 3 blankets.
No 6, missing:	15 wine glasses, jug and basin, 1 blanket, 1 rug.
NORTH END VILLA	
Parlor No 1:	3 cane-seated chairs broken.
No 2, missing:	jug and basin, looking glass, 5 pairs sheets, 2 tablecloths, 6 pillows and slips, 5 toilet covers.
No 3, missing:	4 counterpanes, 12 blankets, 2 bolsters, 2 short pillows, mattress, bolster and pillow.
No 4, missing:	2 bolsters, 2 short pillows.

Kitchen, missing:	4 large dishes, 3 vegetable dishes, 2 dozen plates.
FARM HOUSE	
No 5, missing:	5 blankets
No 7, missing:	3 towels, 3 tablecloths, 2 dinner napkins, 3 pillow slips, 4 bedroom towels.
Kitchen, missing:	2 water cans, 8 small knives, carving knife and fork. 12 knives and forks, 1 fish drainer, 1 china tea pot, 1 metal tea pot

. . .and we say that the value of the effects so deficient and defective is estimated by us at the sum of £101. 19s.

LIVESTOCK   Deficiency of 165 sheep, value estimated at £330.
. . .with respect to the lambs 14 were sold to Benthall in July 1869, and we have been informed by James Darling, the Shepherd employed on the Island, that 50 lambs were born in the year 1870, and 51 in the year 1871 making together 125 lambs, of these we found 51 on the Island leaving 64 lambs deficient which we value at £64. We however found 1 bull not belonging to the Company which we value at £10, also 1 ram value £3, and two milch cows value £28, making together £41 which amount should be deducted from the sum charged against Mr Benthall.

The value of the steamer *Vanderbyl* to be deducted against Mr Benthall for £700.

GRANITE:
During the period of Benthall's possession the following shipments were made:
29 July 1869, 27.17 cwt of pitching per the *Eliza* taken to Barnstaple and sold there
9 September 1869, about 10 tons pitching and 288 lineal feet curbs per the *Eliza* landed at Fremington, taken by barge to Barnstaple, and sold there
31 May 1870, 147 stones curbs, 4 tons broken ends, and other granite shipped per the *Acorn*, with Mr Benthall on board.
13 June 1870, 187 stone curbs containing 640 lineal feet edge flat, 137 cubic feet rough blocks, 5 tons broken refuse landing steps, 14 quoins, shipped per the *Acorn* to Fremington.
12 August 1870, Steps for J Baker & Son, Bideford per *Vanderbyl* with Benthall aboard.
Also 2 cows (1 killed in shipment) and a quantity of hay
Mr Benthall on the island for two weeks.
20-25 August 1870, 2 voyages of the *Vanderbyl* shipped 7 rough blocks 184 cubic feet, 2 scabbled blocks 52 cubic feet, 2 thin blocks, 32 cubic feet, 13 refuse lumps 34 cubic feet, 14 steps 69 lineal feet, 4 landings, 72 superficial feet landings.
Amounts received for sale of granite:
1869 August, 49 cube ft @ 1s. per foot for Bideford £2 9s.1d.
18 cube ft @ 6d. per foot Mr J Baker 9s.
1870 January, 144 superficial @ 6d, Biscuit factory, Barnstaple £3. 14s.
167 ft lineal @ 6d, Ching, Bideford £4. 3s.
February, 16 cube ft @ 1s. Squires, Bideford, 16s.
2 loads spalbs @ 2s. per load, 4s.
March, 112 ft lineal @ 4d. per foot, New, Torrington £1. 17s.
June, 216 cube @ 1s. £10.16s.

July, 160 ft lineal @ 1s 6d. Hamilton, Pilton. £ 4
August, 8 ft lineal @ 1s.6d. Mr Mitchell, Exeter.12 s.
December, 200 ft @ 6d. Mr W. Gould, Barnstaple. £ 5
6ft x 3 x 6 @ 1s. Mr Gould, Barnstaple.18s.
74 ft 6 ins @ 1s. Parson Pickoot, Bickington. £3. 14s.
1870-1871 Barnstaple Commissioners and Bridge Trust,
2 cargoes stone per *Eliza*,   £40.10s.
Less freight £10.10s, discharging £1.12s.6d. £28.   7s.
1871 January, Stone sold to Mr Lancy, Barnstaple. £11.2s.6d.
Less working £ 4 19s.9d. £ 6   2s   9d.
February & March, Stone 447 ft sold to the Mayor of Barnstaple.
@ 1s. per ft. £22. 7s.
February, Stone sold to Helwell of Torrington. £ 6.   9s.
Total value of stone sold £101.19s.7d.
Due from Barnstaple Commissioners for stone sold £7.10s.
No estimate made for profits from farm produce or any other source.

National archives C31/254

*

APPENDIX VI

A LEGAL PRECEDENT

In re Lundy Granite Co; Ex parte Heaven (1871) LR 6 Ch App 462
1871

Representation

* Solicitors: Messrs. Vizard, Crowder, & Co.; Mr. R. Miller.

1. 1871. March 6. LORD ROMILLY, M.R.:- This is an application by the proprietor of Lundy Island for leave to issue a distress upon certain goods of the company which are upon Lundy Island for payment of rent which is admitted to be due to him. The property on which the proprietor of the island wishes to distrain belongs to the company, but it happens to be on land which is leased to another person. The company are not carrying on business, or doing anything which would in any shape make them liable to pay rent, so that there is no debt due from them to the proprietor; but there is property of theirs which is upon the land that is demised, upon which property the landlord, according to the ordinary law of England, unless it is modified by the statutes relating to joint stock companies, is entitled to distrain. The question in this case is, whether he is entitled to distrain upon those goods. In the first place, one very important distinction arises in this case. The distress was put in, or was asked to be put in, which is the same thing, subsequently to the winding-up order. Therefore the cases in which the Court has held that where an execution issues, or the goods are taken, before the winding-up order is made, the Court will not interfere, do not apply. Then, how is Mr. Heaven affected by the Act of Parliament? There are two sections on the subject which are very plain and clear. The first is the 163rd section, which is to this effect: ' Where any company is being wound up by the Court, or subject to the supervision of the Court, any attachment, sequestration, distress, or execution put in force against the estate or effects of the company after the commencement of the winding-up shall be void to all intents.' Without raising any question whether ' being wound up' means before the order or not, it is quite clear that it applies after the winding-up order, and this section says distinctly that the distress ' shall be void to all intents.' The result is, that if that section stood alone the distress cannot be levied. It does not say a distress in respect of any rent due, or anything of that description, but a distress upon the goods of the company. But this section is to be taken in conjunction with the 87th section, which is to this effect: ' When an order has been made for winding up a company under this Act no suit, action, or other proceeding shall be proceeded with or commenced against the company, except with the leave of the Court, and subject to such terms as the Court may impose.' Now, it is quite clear that a distress is a proceeding against the goods of the company, because, if this section does not apply, the other section makes it absolutely void. Therefore the Court may give leave, and also impose such terms as it thinks fit. I am of opinion that the Court has clear jurisdiction to do what it thinks right in this matter. I hold it to be quite clear and certain, that, assuming that the company was the lessee of the applicant, then the Court would stop the distress, and allow the appli-

cant to prove for the amount of rent against the company. That, in fact, was done by me in a previous case. I do not understand that it has been objected to, and I believe that it has always been followed. Mr. Roxburgh, who argued this case with great ingenuity and ability, said that it did not apply to this case, because Mr. Heaven was not a creditor of the company, and could not prove at all in the winding-up. Technically, that may be correct; but, substantially, I do not think it has any weight, because this applicant has a species of lien, according to the English law, unless taken away by this statute, against certain goods of the company, and the Court has the power of saying that he shall not levy a distress upon these goods of the company, or, if he does, he shall levy it upon such terms and conditions as the Court shall direct. I am of opinion that the whole of the principle of this Act, and the reason of these sections, was not to prevent a person from recovering his proper debt against the company, or his proper claim against the company, but to put everybody who had claims upon the company upon an equal footing. It so happens, from the peculiarity of the English law, that a person can distrain upon the goods of the company which happen to be upon the lands of the lessee, though the landlord is, strictly speaking, not a creditor of the company. Yet I am of opinion that he is, for all intents and purposes under this Act, to be treated as in exactly the same situation- that he ought to be put pari passu with all those persons who have any claims upon the company; that he ought not to have any particular or exclusive preference or advantage by reason of the circumstance that he has only incidentally by law a claim upon the property of the company without being a creditor of the company, and that he ought to be put in the same situation as if it were the property of the company. Therefore I am of opinion that the proper order to make on this motion is to say that the distress shall not issue, but that Mr. Heaven shall be at liberty to prove against the company, not as a creditor, but merely to prove to this amount against the company, and that he is to be entitled to receive a dividend pari passu with all the creditors of the company. I think, also, having regard to all the circumstances of this case, that he ought to add his costs of this application to his proof, and prove the whole against the company.
2. 12 W. R. 727; 4 N. R. 127.
3. Law Rep. 9 Eq. 370.
(c) Incorporated Council of Law Reporting for England & Wales

THE APPEAL

462 In re Lundy Granite Company
Court of Appeal in Chancery
10 March 1871
(1870-71) L.R. 6 Ch. App. 462
Sir W. M. James and Sir G. Mellish, L. JJ.
1871 March 10
Company- Winding-up- Rent- Distress- Companies Act, 1862, ss. 87, 163.
Where a company, being equitable owner of a lease, continues after a winding-up order in the occupation of the leaseholds, and leaves goods upon the land, the landlord is not, by sect. 87 or sect. 163 of the Companies Act, 1862, prevented from distraining upon the goods of the company for rent accrued since the winding-up. Orders of the Master of the Rolls discharged.
IN August, 1863, Mr. H. Heaven demised to Mr. McKenna, Lundy Island for seven

or fourteen years, at the yearly rent of £700. Shortly afterwards McKenna agreed to assign the lease to the Lundy Granite Company, Limited, and the company took possession of the island, and continued in possession. On the 19th of November, 1868, an order for winding up the company was made. The official liquidator did not remove the goods of the company from the island, and paid the rent to Mr. Heaven up to the 24th of June, 1869, but apparently for McKenna, and Mr. Heaven seemed *463 not to have recognised the company as tenants. Some negotiations took place between the official liquidator, McKenna, and Mr. Heaven, and some proceedings in Chambers as to a surrender of the lease, and the grant of a new lease to one Benthall, which, however, had no result. There was a considerable amount of property on the island belonging to the company, and the official liquidator proposed to sell this and the other property of the company; whereupon Mr. Heaven, having previously applied to McKenna for the rent, distrained for the rent due to the 25th of December, 1870, McKenna being named in the warrant as the tenant. The property taken under the distress belonged to the company, and the Master of the Rolls, on the 23rd of February, 1871, made an order in the winding-up restraining Mr. Heaven from proceeding. Mr. Heaven then moved for leave to proceed, which was refused by the Master of the Rolls1.
*464
Mr. Heaven appealed from both the orders.
Mr. Roxburgh, Q.C., and Mr. Badcock, for the Appellant:-
Sections 163 and 164 of the Companies Act, 1862, on which the *465 Master of the Rolls went, apply only to creditors of the company. If the landlord was a creditor of the company it would be different, as appears from sect. 87, but he is not; he has nothing to do with the company, and is only proceeding to recover his rent. The statute cannot have been intended to take away the common law rights of the landlord, and to leave him without a remedy: In re Exhall Coal Mining Company2; In re Progress Assurance Company 3.
Mr. Swanston, Q.C., and the Hon. E. Romilly, for the official liquidator:-
There had been negotiations between Mr. Heaven and the official liquidator for the surrender of the lease, and Mr. Heaven knew that the goods belonged to the company. There is no case in which the Court has given leave to a creditor where proceedings had not been begun before the winding-up. The whole scope of the Act is, that creditors shall be put upon an equal footing, and that no one shall be allowed to avail himself of any special rights. This is clearly a distress on the goods of the company, and as such is void under sect. 163; nor is it a case where leave to proceed ought to be given. It makes no difference that the company is not the lessee, as the goods belong to the company, and are protected. The Act could not have intended to place the company in a worse position as lessee than as under lessee. If there had been a lien on the goods before the winding-up, of course it must have been discharged, but this rent has accrued since.
SIR W. M. JAMES, L.J.:-
My opinion is, that the appeal in this case is well founded, and that the orders of the Master of the Rolls cannot stand. Before we consider the application of the 163rd section to distress against a lessee, the goods being on the property, and liable, it may be expedient to consider how it would have been if the case had been *466 between the lessor and the company, in which case it is settled that the distress issued against the company is not made void by sect. 163, but is, like every other proceeding, subject to the power of the Court, to deal with according as the

Court think right. The Court has dealt with it by putting the landlord, who has not forfeited his right, in the same position as any other creditor, as he may go in and prove, which appears to be the result of what has been done in this case.

But in some cases between the landlord and the company, if the company for its own purposes, and with a view to the realization of the property to better advantage, remains in possession of the estate, which the lessor is therefore not able to obtain possession of, common sense and ordinary justice require the Court to see that the landlord receives the full value of the property. He must have the same rights as any other creditor, and if the company choose to keep the estates for their own purposes, they ought to pay the full value to the landlord, as they ought to pay any other person for anything else, and the Court ought to take care that he receives it.

There is nothing to shew that Mr. Heaven has in any way deprived himself of his right to receive the full amount of the rent. He appears to have been ready to make any reasonable arrangement, and there seems to be nothing to affect his right to do what was best for himself.

That being so, we must consider what is the position of a stranger under the Act, the landlord having the power of distress against the tenant:- [His Lordship read the 163rd section.] Now these words cannot be taken as meaning that the distress is to be absolutely void to all intents, or else the Court would have no jurisdiction to allow the landlord to proceed; and, moreover, a distress would be void as against another lessee if the goods of the company were left on the land and were taken. But it is impossible that a distress on land can be void merely because the company have goods there.

In no other part of the Act is any person dealt with except the company, its creditors, and its contributories. The sole object of the Act was to make an equitable provision in the nature of a bankruptcy for the distribution of the effects of the company *467 amongst the persons entitled, but not to alter any other rights which they might acquire during the winding-up. If the official liquidator chooses to leave goods in the order and disposition of a bankrupt, there is nothing, as far as I can see, to prevent the assignee from taking them; and so if he leaves goods in a house where a landlord has a right to distrain, the official liquidator must take the consequences. It must be the true meaning of the Act to consider these provisions as confined to proceedings by a creditor of the company against the goods of the company; and the Act must be read according to the manifest intention, which could not have been that during the many years over which the winding-up may extend the Court should have power to interfere with the rights of every one who happened to have goods of the company in his possession. The landlord has a right to proceed against his tenant, and against the goods of every stranger which happen to be upon the land, and subject to distress.

As a general rule, I should have no hesitation in granting leave to a landlord to pursue his rights by distress for rent accrued during the time when the official liquidator chooses to leave the goods on the land.

SIR G. MELLISH, L.J.:-

I agree. If the official liquidator, for the convenience of the winding-up, does not surrender the lease, but continues to keep possession for the purpose of obtaining a better price for the goods, the landlord should not be deprived of his right to recover his rent.

It is a question of general importance whether this section relates only to distress against the company, that is to say, where the company is the debtor, or extends, as has been contended, to all cases of distress. The landlord is, by the law of this country, entitled to take as a security for his rent the goods upon his land, whomsoever they belong to. Then, was it intended to deprive the landlord of that right if the goods happened to belong to a company under liquidation.

It would be very extraordinary if the Legislature had deprived the landlord of that right without clear and express words, and *468 without giving him any compensation. The right to prove debts is confined to creditors of the company, and it this section makes this distress void, I do not see what power the Court would have to say that the landlord has any right to prove for his debt. It would be very extraordinary if, during the whole time of a liquidation, the, liquidator might make any agreement with any insolvent tenant, and keep the goods on the land without any risk. The difficulty is not met by saying that the landlord can get leave to proceed under sect. 87, for that section is confined to proceedings against the company:- [His Lordship read the section]. This throws a good deal of light upon sect. 163, and when we look at the place where sect. 163 comes in, it is seen clearly to deal with the rights of creditors under the winding-up. As to all the words except the word ' distress,' there can be no doubt, and I think that they all in some way relate to proceedings by a creditor of the company against the company, in which the company would be a Defendant. It was not the intention of the Legislature to deal at all with the rights of a landlord, who may be a total stranger to the company, and may not know to whom the goods belong.

It was said that Mr. Heaven was a party to the proceedings between the company and the proposed new lessee, but that gives no equitable right against him.

We must discharge the two orders. Mr. Heaven will have his costs below, and the official liquidator will have his out of the estate..

SUMMARY OF THE FINDINGS

Andrew Burke

Because the Company was not the Tenant under the Lease (which had not been formally assigned to the Company, and therefore remained between Heaven and McKenna) the Company was not legally liable to Heaven for payment of rent and other monies due under the Lease.

Faced with arrears, Mr Heaven, as lessor, wanted to distrain (i.e. seize and sell) the goods upon the land which was subject to the Lease, irrespective of whether those goods belonged to the Tenant (McKenna) or the Company. The right to distrain is an ancient common law right, and the Counsel for Heaven argued before Lord Romilly M.R. that it should apply in this case, irrespective of the fact that the goods in question belonged not to the Tenant but to a corporate body - the Company.

It should be remembered that the Companies Act of 1862 was very new law at the time that the case came before the Courts. Lord Romilly M.R., in the Court of the first instance, was therefore having to consider the relationship of the new Act to the facts of the case. He decided, not surprisingly, that as the effect of the distrain would be 'a proceeding against the goods of the Company,' it would either be void under section 163 of the Act, or in the alternative, that under section 87 of the Act it could not be proceeded with without the leave of the Court, and in effect he declined to give such leave, and refused to allow the distress on the grounds that doing so would have given Heaven an advantage or preference against the creditors and members with claims against the Company, to which advantage he, Heaven, was not entitled.

Four days later the Court of Appeal reversed this decision, finding - in essence - that Parliament had not intended the Act to deprive a Lessor of the ancient right to distrain goods upon his land for a breach of Lease. If the Tenant had been the Company the distress would not have been void, according to the Court of Appeal, and could have proceeded even during the liquidation, with the leave of the Court.

That being the case, in a situation where the Tenant was not the Company, it was clearly the case that distress should be allowed, and the fact that the Liquidator had - for his own purposes with a view to maximising potential returns in the liquidation - left Company goods on the land should not prevent the Lessor from proceeding with the distress, particularly where in practice the continued occupation of the land by the Company prevented the Lessor from otherwise disposing of it.

Fig. 96 *Lord Romilly - Master of the Rolls 1851-1873*
(Rothwell collection)

APPENDIX VII

1871 CENSUS RETURNS FOR LUNDY

No. of Schedule	Road, Street, &c, No or Name of House	In-habit-ed	Uninh abited (U), or building (B)	Name and Surname of each Person	Relation to Head of Family	Condi tion	Age of Males	Age of Fem-ales	Rank, Profession or Occupation	Where Born
1	Farm Houses	I	U	Frederick Wilkins	Head	Mar	45		Manager of Quarries & Farm, Registrar of Births & Deaths. 1924 acres employing 5 Masons and 1 Workman	Maiden Hill, Middlesex
	Manager's House	I	U							
	Stores & Bakehouses	I	U							
2	Garden Cottages			James Darling	Occupier	Unm.	60		Shepherd	Bristol, Somersetshire
	Store Keeper's House			William Dennis	Boarder	Unm.	40		Farmer	Buckland, Devonshire
3	The Villa	I		William H Heaven	Head	Wid.	71		Landowner	Glostershire, Lower Easton
				Hudson G Do	Son	Unm	45		In Holy Orders, without care of Souls	Somertsetshire, Pilton
				Cecilia H Do	Dau.	Unm		40		France, British Subject
				Amelia A Do	Dau	Unm		37		Somersetshire, Walton
				Marion E Do	Dau in Law	W		29		London
				Marion CH Do	Grand Dau			9	Scholar	New South Wales, Sydney
				Walter CH Do	Grand Son		5		Scholar	New South Wales, Sydney
				Elise Holm	Gover-ness	Unm		18	Governess	Hamburg
				Charles W Treleaven	Domestic Serv't	Unm	18		Domestic Serv't	Cornwall, Can
				Margaret Jeffery	Domestic Serv't	Unm		44	Domestic Serv't	North Devon, Hopstone
				Eliza Dolling	Domestic Serv't	Unm		46	Domestic Serv't	Somersetshire, Taunton
				Susan Hopper	Domestic Serv't	Unm		35	Domestic Serv't	North Devon, Woolfardisworthy
4	The Castle No.1	I		Thomas Withacombe	Head	Mar	50		? Laborer	North Devon, Landkey
				Ann Do	Wife	Mar		57		North Devon, Exford

#	Dwelling		Name	Relation	Cond	Age M	Age F	Occupation	Birthplace
5	Do		Henry Board	Lodger	Unm	39		Mason Laborer	Somersetshire, Hunts Field
6	Do	I	Susanna Spearman	Head	W		67	Householder	North Devon, Hartland
7	The Castle No.2		Joseph Dark	Head	Mar	35		Carpenter	Devonshire, Parkham
			Mary Do	Wife	Mar		35		Devonshire, Hartland
			Margaret Do	Dau			9		Devonshire, Woolfardisworthy
			Dora Do	Dau			7		Devonshire, Parkham
			Ellen Do	Dau			5		Devonshire, Parkham
			Florence Do	Dau			11mnths		Devonshire, Woolfardisworthy
8			William Cichard	Lodger	Mar	54		Master Mariner	Devonshire, Northam
	No.3	U							
9	Light House	I	Jeremiah G Howgego	Head	Mar	57		Principal Light Keeper	Essex, Harwich
			Elizabeth Do	Wife	Mar		47		Sussex, Nattenden
			Harriet E	Dau			12		Channel Islands, Alderney
			Harvey E	Son		6			Bristol Channel, Lundy
10			William J Rees	Head	Mar	25		Light Keeper	Wales, Caldy Island
			Mary A Do	Wife	Mar		23		Lincolnshire, Boston
			Mary T Do	Dau			2		Devonshire, Braunton
			William J Do	Son		9mnths			Cornwall, Sennon Cove
11	Light House Cottage	I	John J Charener	Head	Mar	32		Light Keeper	London
			Pheobe Do	Wife	Mar		30		Wales,Foxhall, Burton parish
			Mary E Do	Dau			8		Lancashire, Liverpool
			Rosa E Do	Dau			6		Devonshire, Plymouth
			Augusta E Do	Dau			4		Wales, Caldy Island
			Arthur W Do	Son		3			Wales, Caldy Island
			John J Do	Son		16mths			Bristol Channel, Lundy Island

151

12	Fog Station	I	Thomas S Lee	Head	Mar	56		Principal Gunner	Devonshire, Clovelly
			Mary A Do	Wife	Mar	26	5		Devonshire, Swimbridge
			Anne W Do	Dau			5		Bristol Channel, Lundy Island
			Elizabeth L Do	Dau			3		Bristol Channel, Lundy Island
			William J Do	Son		1			Bristol Channel, Lundy Island
13			John Blackmore	Head	Mar	31		Gunner	Somerset, Spaxton
			Mary A Do	Wife	Mar		37		Buckinham, Gt Kimbles
			Mary E Do	Dau			9		Bristol Channel, Lundy Island
			Anne L Do	Dau			7		Devonshire, Clovelly
			Caroline R Do	Dau			6		Bristol Channel, Lundy Island
			Walter J Do	Son		3			Bristol Channel, Lundy Island
			Thomas H Do	Son		2			Bristol Channel, Lundy Island
			Edward H Do	Son		11 mths			Devonshire, Bideford
	Barracks No.s 1-4	I U							
	" 5	U							
	" 6	U							
	Iron House	U							
	Golden Square No.1	U							
	2	U							
	3	U							
	4	U							
	5	U							
	6	U							
14	Sea View Terrace No.1	I	Obediah Johns	Head	Mar	30		Laborer	Devonshire, Bradbury
			Elizabeth Do	Wife	Mar		30		Devonshire, Woolfardisworthy
			Charlotte Do	Dau			10		Devonshire,

Address	No.	U/I	Name	Relation	Status	M	F	Occupation	Birthplace
			Charles Do	Son		8			Devonshire, Bradbury
			Elizabeth Do	Dau			7		Devonshire, Bradbury
			Obediah Do	Son		5			Devonshire, Bradbury
			Richard Do	Son		3			Devonshire, Bradbury
Do	2	U							
Do	3	U							
Do	4	U							
Do	5	U							
Do	6	U							
Do	7	U							
Do	8	U							
Quarter Wall No.1	1		Henry Northover	Occupier	Unm	22		Quarryman	Jersey, British Subject
			Richard Walters	Boarder	Unm	24		Quarryman	Molton Abbott, Devonshire
Do	2	U							
Do	3	U							
Do	4	I/U							
Outside Quarter Wall No 1		U							
	2	U							
	3	U							
	4	U							
	5	U							
Hospital		U							
Bel View Villas No1		U							
	2	U							
	3	U							

(Row marker: 15)

APPENDIX VIII

Prospectus of the
LUNDY GRANITE COMPANY Ltd.

MEMORANDUM OF PROSPECTUS

OF

THE LUNDY GRANITE COMPANY, LIMITED.

This Company is formed for the purpose of working the extensive Granite Quarries of Lundy Island.

The limited area from which Granite is obtainable in Great Britain, and the high commercial value of the stone, equal to from 27s. to 80s. a ton, render the present undertaking a very remarkable one.

Lundy Island, which is situated about twelve miles from the coast of North Devon, may be described as a vast mass of granite, rising, with almost perpendicular elevation, from the sea, to a height of more than four hundred feet, being about three miles in length and having an extent of surface land approaching 2000 acres

The specimens of Granite from the Island of 1862 received from the commissioners an HONORABLE MENTION OF THE FIRST CLASS; and the colour and texture were much admired by some of the best judges of the stone. The Island contains many kinds of Granite; some of them are very fine in the grain, and capable of taking a high polish.

Whilst there is always a large and increasing demand for this valuable stone, there is, just now, being created a most extensive requirement for it, for the construction of the Coast Fortifications, and the projected Thames Embankment. The supply obtainable from Lundy Island may be stated to be practically unlimited.

There is a natural Harbour on the east coast of the Island, where the water is of considerable depth, perfectly protected from the prevailing winds, so that vessels moored alongside can take in cargoes of stone, quarried from the adjoining cliffs, with the greatest facility.

From the peculiar advantage, that the place of production is also the place of shipment, with no heavy expenditure to be incurred in lifting the blocks from the quarries and in land-carriage, it is estimated that the cost of producing the stone will be less than that of any other Granite quarry in the Kingdom.

It should be particularly observed, that although the Granite of Lundy has been shown to be of a very superior class, yet, as the Quarries have not been sufficiently opened to admit of the selection of the best specimens of the stone, there is every probability that when a lower depth shall have been reached, the White Granite will prove to be of a kind which cannot be equalled in texture and purity by any other in Great Britain. It is so well-suited for architectural purposes, that it is reasonable to expect that it will meet with, and probably create, a considerable demand for its use in the construction of many of the large and costly edifices which are at all times being erected in the Metropolis.

From the foregoing considerations as to the abundance and quality of the stone, and the comparative cheapness with which it can be quarried and shipped, it may be stated that the undertaking holds out the prospect of a very remunerative return on the capital to be employed; and if, with these advantages can be combined that of cheap freight, it will be admitted that every condition will exist, under good management, for achieving a great commercial success.

A glance at the map will show that the Island lies in the track of the coal trade, between the ports of South Wales and those on the southern coast, the Irish ports and the ports of London; and it occupies such a position with reference to the navigation of the Bristol and Irish Channels, which are much frequented by vessels in search of freights, that a supply of shipping to carry the stone to London and other ports may be confidently anticipated.

The absence of port dues at Lundy, and the facilities for loading with promptitude, will ensure, as a natural result of the competition which exists amongst the numerous coasters, a sufficient supply of ships at all seasons and at ordinary freights.

Another mode of carrying the stone must be mentioned. The port of Instow can be reached in four hours from Lundy, and from that point the Granite can be conveyed by railway, in any direction. The use of a steam-tug would render the sea-passage practicable in any state of the wind; and, if the trade to London can, as it is believed, be made very considerable, it would be to the interest of the South-Western railway Company to reduce their tariff so as to compete with the ship-owner.

The following estimate of prices and cost of producing and carrying the stone will indicate the rate of profits to be anticipated:

Average price per ton
1st Class
Fine Granite for Monumental work in Cemeteries,
Columns, Statues, and other high-class work   -   -   -   50s. to 80s.
2nd Class – For Docks, Wharves, &c.   -   -   -   -   40s. to 50s.
3rd Class. – For Paving Kerbs   -   -   -   -   27s. to 40s.

It is difficult to calculate an average profit on the 1st Class, but the price mostly includes the cost of cutting according to design, and polishing, which would be executed by the Company at the Quarries, or at their depot near the railway station. It may, however, be stated that this branch of the trade admits of indefinite extension, and is the most profitable.

In the 2nd Class, the following is an approximate estimate:

Average price per ton -	-	£2 5 0
Coat of raising and working in block and scalpings for masons -		0 12 0
Payment to the Lord of the Manor	-	0 1 0
Freight to London	-	0 9 0
Incidental expanses	-	0 1 0
		£1 3 0
Profit		£1 2 0

In the 3rd Class, the average price would be, say	-	£1 13 6
The cost of quarrying and scalping is estimated at not more than Half of the above rates, and including payment to The Lord of the Soil, would amount to - - - -		0 6 6
Freight to London		0 9 0
Incidental expenses		0 1 0
		0 16 6
Profit		£0 17 0

The farm, which is let with the quarries, covers an area of about 1,400 acres. It is capable of producing considerable profit under judicious management, and its possession by the Company will secure advantages as regards the carrying on of the Quarrying operations without hindrance, and the supply of the produce to the workman at a moderate cost.

The Quarries of the Island together with the Farm have been secured by the Company from the lessee on the most advantageous terms; namely, for a payment of 1s. per ton for the granite in block, the Company guaraunteeing [sic] to raise or pay for at least 4000 tons annually, 6d. per ton when prepared on the island for kerbs or pitching, and 3d. per ton for rubble, with a rent of £500 a-year for the farm, which is only equivalent to the agricultural value of the land. These are in fact the terms on which the Lessee holds them from the Lord of the soil, but it is stipulated that he shall be entitled to half the profits realized in excess of 310 per cent. per annum on the paid-up capital.

Under this arrangement, if only 10 per cent. is earned, the lessee (who sells to the Company) receives no dividend. If 20 per cent. is earned, the Shareholders will receive £15 per cent., and the lessee £5 percent. If £30 percent. is earned, the Shareholders will receive £20 per cent. and the lessee £10 per cent., and progressively in like manner. But it is agreed that when the Shareholders shall have been paid in Dividends and Bonuses sums equivalent to the whole of their paid-up Capital, and interest thereon at the rate of £10 per cent. per annum, the lessee shall be entitled to commute his rights into shares of the Company, in the ratio of nine shares to the lessee for every ten held by the other Shareholders.

It is further agreed that the lessee shall reserve the right to quarry stone for constructing a Harbour and Breakwater at Lundy Island; also that monies payable under any arrangement with the Government for the privilege of quarrying stone on the Island for public works, shall be divided in equal shares between the lessee and the Company.

No payments will be made to promoters, except in respect of actual expenses, which are guaranteed not to exceed £500, including costs of every description.

CONDENSED REPORTS REFLECTING THE PROPERTIES OF LUNDY GRANITE

From Robert Etheridge, Esq., Geological Museum, Jermyn Street.

An exhaustless quantity of Granite of various degrees of compactness and composition occurs on this island, which indeed is almost entirely composed of this important and durable stone, chiefly of a good white colour, and a considerable quantity fine grained, and of even texture, taking a good polish, and free from iron-pyrites and other oxidisable minerals, which are detrimental to the durability of the Granite upon exposure, or when used for its required purposes.

On the eastern side of the island, in particular faces or cliffs, from 100 to 300 feet in height, composed of extremely dense or solid Granite, which are natural quarries standing out seaward, and with sufficient water for the accommodation of the largest vessels at all stages of the tides.

The Granite belongs to that group containing hornblende and much silica, an important feature in its durability for heavy structures, and these are associated with other varieties, and may be worked together. Brazen Ward and Ganet's Comb [sic] are the most eligible positions for quarries, the latter affording every facility for the establishment of extensive quarries and shipping accommodation, where the finest and largest blocks can be hewn and worked and then passed to the shipping stages beneath.

*

From Mr. R. D. Gould, Architect and Surveyor, Barnstaple
I have no hesitation in saying that some of the Lundy Granite is equal to the best Haytor, and superior to much of what I have obtained from Penrhyn, Cheesering, and other Cornish Quarries; there is one bed which, from its fine texture, is adapted for the delicate mouldings, and that class of work which it is difficult to develop in such a material as Granite. I am certain that Granite can be brought from Lundy Island to this place with the widest allowance for quarrying, freight, &c., and rendered at a price far below what we are now paying.

*

From Messrs. H. Poole & Son, Statuaries, Great Smith Street
We have been required to give our opinion of the Lundy Granite, of which we polished several specimens for inspection. We think the stone is very desirable as a building stone, by reason of its great durability, of which the specimens exhibit good promise; also, for the agreeable colour, being very light, and, also, for the comparative ease with which it may be wrought. We have no doubt, if it can be brought to market, at a price per foot cube not exceeding the ordinary Granite, it will, in many cases, have a preference especially for ornamental purposes.

*

From Samuel Trickett, Esq., of Millwall

I have examined the Granite on the north-west and north-east of the island and Gannet's Cove, and am of the opinion that there is abundance of good merchandisable Granite, of fine close texture, and good colour, and quality, such as would command a high price for Cemetery purposes and works of art. The quarries are not sufficiently opened to allow a correct judgment to be formed, but from indications, I am of opinion that the fine rock will be found to run from the east to the west of the island. I have no doubt that, with judicious management, a large and profitable business may be done.

*

From Messrs. Easton and son, Granite Merchants, Exeter and Haytor Granite Works

The Island of Lundy, which I have visited, would be the cheapest place in England to open Granite Quarries, because the Granite is on the surface; there is no head of any consequence to be taken away, and the place is well adapted for a ship to load as there is a natural formed Harbour, where ships could load without difficulty; the Haytor Granite Company and others have a great deal of land carriage before getting to a port or rail. The cost of quarrying at Lundy would be 6d. a foot cube, in blocks from 6 to 40 feet. This is after the quarry is opened, which could be done for a trifle. We should not recommend you to dress works at all; merely sell it scappled, and no Company in England could compete with you.

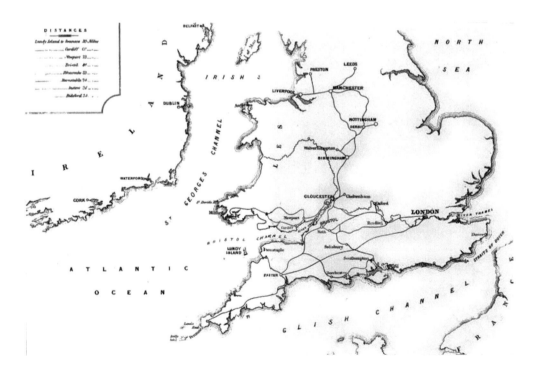

APPENDIX IX

Extract from the Prospectus of
THE LUNDY ISLAND & MAINLAND QUARRIES LIMITED

The Quarries, embracing an area of 5 acres, are on the east side of the island, where there is splendid anchorage in deep water at all tides, and are held for a term of 21 years from December 8th 1896, renewable for a further term of 21 years, and are estimated to contain not less than:

50 millions of tons or upwards of 800 million cubic feet of Granite
of a high class for a durability, purity of colour, and fineness of grain.

The rent and Royalties payable under the lease are as follows:

A Dead Rent of £100 per annum merging into Royalties.
A Royalty of 2d. a ton for Rubble, Waste, &c.
A Royalty of 3d. per ton for stones not exceeding 10 cubic feet.
A Royalty of 6d. per ton for all other stone.

The Lessor has agreed that if in any year sufficient stone is not worked for the Royalties to amount to the Dead Rent such deficiency may be made up in the immediately succeeding year.

His Majesty's Government have in hand and in contemplation important Harbour Works, Dockyards, and Barracks, that will for many years require large quantities of Granite, dressed and unwrought.

The Mersey Docks and Harbour Board propose to spend £3,500,000 in the extension of their docks and other works. The Bristol Dock Committee have just determined to enlarge their Dock and Wharf accommodation at Avonmouth at a cost of £2,000,000, whilst Ilfracombe will probably require considerable tonnage of Granite for the development of their Pier and Harbour. Very important Dock extensions are also to be proposed to be carried out at Swansea at a cost of nearly £2,000,000, and a Harbour of Refuge at the mouth of the Bristol Channel is contemplated.

The foregoing are mentioned as indicating the extraordinary requirements for Granite, but in addition to this there is the ordinary trade every year rapidly increasing in extent through Granite becoming more general in the construction of Public and Private Buildings. No less than 60 Testimonials have been received from Architects, Engineers, and Builders expressing approval for Lundy Granite. Messrs. David Kirkaldy & Son, the well-known experts, report as to the results of experiments to ascertain the resistance to thrusting stress of 3 samples of Lundy Island Granite:

Mean, 28,403 lbs. to the square inch;
Or 1,500 tons to the square foot.
The above Certificate compares very
favourably with:

Aberdeen Grey	10,900 lbs. to sq. inch.
Cornish	14,000 lbs. to sq. inch.
Mount Sorrell	12,800 lbs. to sq. inch

vide Molesworth's Tables.

In addition to Quarrying it is intended to manufacture Artificial Flags for pavements as well as other concrete work, there being good gravel obtainable at small cost for mixing with the crushed Granite. The sale of these goods is increasingly large and very remunerative.

ESTIMATE OF RECEIPTS AND EXPENDITURE.

Assuming an Output of 10,000 tons of Granite per Annum measuring 14 cubic feet per ton, equal to 140,000 cubic feet.

	£	s	d		£	s	d
140,000 cubic feet of Granite at an average of 1s. 6d. per foot	10,500	0	0	Royalties on 10,000 tons of Granite at an average of 4d. per ton	166	13	4
				Rates and Taxes	NIL		
				Quarrying at 7s. per ton	3,500	0	0
				Machinery, Tools and Blastings at 5s. per ton	2,500	0	0
				Land Carriage	NIL		
				Loading Costs at 6d. per ton	250	0	0
				Wharfage and Port Dues	NIL		
					7,416	13	4
	£10,500	0	0	Profit (gross)	3,063	6	8
					10,500	0	0
Profit (gross) Brought down	3,083	6	8	Cost of Administration	700	0	0
				Sinking Fund to redeem Purchase Money by 37 Annual Installments	81	1	8
				Profit (net)	2,802	5	0
	£3,083	6	8		£3,083	6	8

Shewing a return of over 23 per cent. Upon a Capital of £10,000

From the above return Income Tax and Bonus, or Exertion money to Workmen, will have to be deducted, which together will it is estimated, reduce the net return to 20 percent.

CERTIFICATE

To the Directors of THE LUNDY ISLAND AND MAINLAND QUARRIES, LIMITED.

GENTLEMEN – I am enabled to state from my personal knowledge of the Granite Quarries (numbering four) on Lundy Island, that a very excellent Granite (samples of which, polished and otherwise, I have in my possession) has been, and can be obtained there very cheaply.

The opinion I have of these quarries being worked in a profitable manner, I have shown on the enclosed assumed Balance Sheet of Receipts for an Output of 140,000 cubic feet per annum. The items therein stated will cover all expenses, and upon a Capital of £10,000 will give a return of over 23 per cent.

I am, Gentlemen, your obedient Servant,
ROBT. H. TAYLOR, A.M.I.C.E. & M.I.M.E., &c

5, MAISON DIEU ROAD, DOVER *February, 1902*

THE
Lundy Island & Mainland Quarries,
LIMITED

Report from Mr. Kyffin Freeman, F.G.S, F.S.S.

GENTLEMEN

In accordance with instructions received, I have paid two visits to Lundy Island to inspect and report on the Granite Quarries.

I was also instructed to consider and report, from my practical experience in working quarries, whether this property offered a fair field for commercial enterprise that would be profitable to investors.

On my first visit I limited my enquiries to the quality of the granite, and to the probable extent of the Quarries. On my second visit I spent three days in a careful inspection of each of the four Quarries, and to confirm my judgement as to the wisest way of working the granite. I was accompanied by one of the most competent and successful managers of Quarry operations in the United Kingdom. I also had levels and soundings taken in connection with the proposed system of shipping the granite, and in the consideration of this matter, I had the advantage of the co-operation of Mr. M. Noel Ridley, A.M.I.C.E., of Westminster, who has had considerable experience in Pier construction on our coasts. I had also the help of Mr. T. H. Fishwick, Lloyds Agent, Appledore, who from his experience in connection with the Trinity Corporation's recent erection of Lighthouses on the Island, has full knowledge of the tides, currents, and prevailing winds, which you would have to contend with.

There are nearly 50,000 superficial feet of workable quarry face in the four quarries; and not less than 17,000 superficial feet of cleared ground available for the construction of Workshops and the erection of Machinery that may be required for Masons, Blacksmiths etc.

I have elsewhere given details of each of the four Quarries; suggestions as to the plan of operations; the best system of shipping the rock; and probable financial result.

> 1st. I report that the Granite is of a high class character for Engineering and Architectural purposes, and that the quantity is *practically inexhaustible*.
> 2nd. The proposed Aerial Cable-way will provide the cheapest and the most efficient mode of transport.
> 3rd. A regular and increasing output for shipment should be maintained and no rubble or waste tips allowed.

I subsequently inspected the other Quarries on the Mainland, as set forth in my supplementary report, and if they can be obtained at or near the price at which I have valued them, they will, in my opinion, prove profitable, and be a distinct advantage to the Granite trade in doing business with Engineers, Contractors, and Merchants.

I am of the opinion that if the various Quarries are worked on the lines laid down, a dividend of from 10 to 15 per cent may be anticipated.

Yours Faithfully,

T. KYFFIN FREEMAN
St. Pancras, London, and St. Breward, Cornwall.   Fellow of the Geological Society

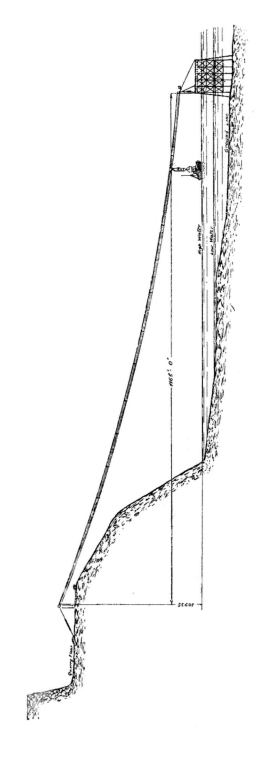

APPENDIX X

Extracts from a report upon the viability of quarrying granite on 'X' (Lundy).
Commissioned by The Right Hon. Baron Rhondda of Llanwern
Presented by Arthur M. Leon, Architect and Engineering Surveyor to the Stacey Estate,
March 20th 1916

THE GRANITE QUARRIES

No. 1.   Very little worked, inferior, and pitched against the workings.
No. 2.   Ditto, as No. 1.
No. 3.   Is distinctly better, and I believe contains a bed of Porphyry about 5ft-0 thick. It is difficult to speak with any certainty the bed being about eighty feet above where I stood, and the face, after forty years, badly weather stained. The pitch of the beds were against the workings more or less, and this makes it more costly to obtain and work.

Exhibit No. 3, marked P. No. 3 by me is Porphyry a fine Granite suitable for Engineering and Architectural work, & possibly road metalling, but on the latter and both issues it should be tested, I would suggest by Mr H.B. Milner, B.A.F.G.S. Sedgwick Museum of Geology, Cambridge, who should inspect the Quarries and take his own samples. I am in doubt as to whether this Elvan is of sufficiently Basalt nature for Road metalling. It is very fine grained close textured Granite, and very hard, but I fear when crushed will make much dust and therefore not be suitable for metalling, being petrologically, I think, Porphyry, Quartz dyke. I was unable to come across a fine Basalt Elvan, but the inspection in the absence of suitable tackle was somewhat cursory. I feel sure there must be many suitable road metals there.

No. 4. Is a splendid quarry, with Granite equal to any I have ever seen, and suitable for all purposes. The dead work is done and the place is ready for working. It has, however, been hacked about by amateur Quarrying, but a months working would square this up. If there is a Basalt Elvan here, I would not work any Quarry but this. Its pitches generally are level, or falling towards the workings. It is an ideal quarry. The Granite is of a muscovite and felspar class, evenly worked, and very effective for treatment.

   Dealing with the component parts forming the Geological and Mineralogical survey of this Granite, Various Professors of eminence have dealt extensively with same, at Lundy. A clear treatise by W.F.P. Macintosh (poss. McIntoe) B., Sc., Royal Scottish Museum, and T.C.F. Hall, F.G.S., read in June 1912, at the Geological School of Mining, I send you, and this Scientific Research is well worth your Lordship's while to study. The Exhibit is marked X7. It is interesting to note that in 1870, S.G. Percival referred to Lundy Granite as being similar in components to Mourne Mountains, which are, I believe, in Galway, Ireland. A book out of print throws, I believe, much light on Lundy. Possibly, it would be in The National Museum. It is called *Chanter's History of Lundy*, Manuscript 1830, by Dr Clay, of Manchester. [sic]
I believe there are many Minerals at Lundy. Copper, and perhaps, Tin, but these like the topaz, are probably of such small quantities as to have no real value. Turning back to the Commercial side, I consider there is about 60 acres of Granite on the East Side, and through to the West parallel just South of the Cheeses.
This really is an inexhaustible field, being over 60 million tons.
As to Lundy, the various pitches of the rock suggests a Volcanic origin, of the Dark Ages. To me its shellet on the South and South east, distinctly resembles and connects itself to Ilfracombe, ...whilst North and West couples itself to Cornwall.
The Shellet is slaty, and the tempests and Father Time are causing the Sea to make inroads into same. I should say many thousands of tons have fallen away during the last fifteen years, and this will continue.
The financial result of a Granite Works with expenditure to the best of my belief would be as follows, subject to the conditions named therein.

ESTIMATE OF RECEIPT AND EXPENDITURE

Assuming an output of 21,000 Tons of Granite, half Roadstone, half blocks, per annum necessary [here 'necessary' is crossed out and, what appears to be 'manageable' or possibly 'theoretical' inserted by hand], 14 cubic feet per ton, the whole equal to 281, 400 cubic ft. Estimated output 500 tons per week, at 42 working weeks, per year, output would be 21,000 tons per year.

	£ s d		£ s d
Half above amount in estimated roadstone, at 5/6 a ton	2887 – 10 - 0	Royalties at 4d per ton on 21,000 tons. Rates and taxes. Nil.	350 - 0 - 0
140,700 c.ft. block Granite (10,500 tons) at 2/3 a c.ft.	15828 – 15 - 0	Quarrying and Crushing roadstone at 3/- a ton on 10,500 tons	1575 - 0 - 0
Gross Sales.	**£18716 - 5 - 0**	Quarrying on blocks at 14/- a ton, on 10,500 tons.	6325 - 0 - 0
	£4,235 - 0 - 0	Machinery, tools, blasting at 5/- per ton, on 10,500 tons of blocks.	2625 - 0 - 0
	1400 - 0 - 0	Do. Do. as last roadstone at 1/- a ton.	525 - 0 - 0
		Land carriage. Nil. Loading cost, 9d a ton, on 21,000 tons.	787 - 0 - 0
		Incidentals at 2/- a ton, on 21,000 tons:	2100 - 0 - 0
Gross Profit	£4235 - 0 - 0	Wharfage & Port dues at 2d a ton, on 21,000 tons.	175 - 0 - 0
		Working Expend.	£14462 -10 – 0
		Gross Profit.	4253 - 15 - 0
			£18716 - 5 - 0
		Cost of Administration. Sinking Fund to redeem Capital expenditure of £20,000 at 2½%. Compound Int. in 27 yrs.	1400 - 0 - 0
			500 - 0 - 0
		Income Tax, Est.: 2/6 in the s. on nett. Profit.	294 - 0 - 0
			2194 - 0 - 0
Gross Profit Brt. Down	£4235 - 0 - 0	Nett Profit.	2059 - 0 - 0
			£4235 - 0 - 0

The above shows approximated dividend of 9% on Capital of £20,000 after deductions for Income Tax and substantial allowances generally.

NOTE: This is provided a market is found for output; further provided delivery is accepted, loaded in boat at Lundy.

Approximated estimate for machinery, Aerial Conveyor, Iron Buildings, and execution to perform the above quarrying,

	£20,000 - 0 - 0
Capital to run the Works, extra, say	4,000 - 0 - 0
Total.	£24,000 - 0 - 0

The Roadstone is priced at 5/6 a ton in boat at Lundy. Freight of boat paid by Public Authorities. If the freight is more than 3/6 a ton, we should be out of the competition for Roadstone, (more or less). These calculations are based on trade being normal after the War, and rates of Wages, material and plant not exceeding $12\frac{1}{2}$% on pre-war conditions.

If it is intended to load ships in all states of weather, it would be necessary to have a Breakwater wall about 250 ft long as indicated by Red circular line on large ordnance.

At low water there is about three fathoms. The spring tide rises about 32 ft above this. The cost of such a Breakwater would be approx. £6000, but this I think might be obviated, and is not to be taken into account. At present, I believe ships standing off in Lundy roads for a day on time, and even perhaps a few hours, might be loaded by an Aerial Ropeway most times, except a Hard East or North East.

Lundy Granite is no experiment, it has great name, and has been used in big works, and big experts speak well of it, (see prospectuses and reports thereon).

NOTE: As to the State of the Granite industry, commercially, pre-war days, I send you a book, Exhibit marked 'X8' on Cornish Granite, and refer your Lordship to pages 17 and 18 underlined, please read.

A question of some 25 or more Cottages for workmen would be more or less self supporting, I have not dwelt on same. They would probably cost £200 each.

ON EARLY PRODUCE.

As recorded on the 8th March it was blowing a bitter gale hard East and perishingly keen on the table land, and heavy wind. This day I inspected the quarries on the East side lands, As we descended to the quarries and walked along such side lands, the wind absolutely disappeared , and it was fairly warm. The descent was gradual and about 120'– 0'. It seemed strange such a change, but I attribute it to the rugged coast line and jutting headlands, breaking up the wind, which must have been striking hard against the East side, from water mark for say 100 ft altitude, then bounded off and re-vollied on the table land and probably fifty feet or more down same. At all events, it was calm and warm. Apple trees were growing, rhododendrons, heather, brooms, gorse, & various wild plants and daffodils were in bloom, and had been, so I was told, for some weeks.

Like everything else, these side lands have run wild, but I believe early produce and flowers could be cultivated. I do not believe it would be as early as Jersey or Scilly, because the yearly result of the Temperature Chart shows 4% colder, and throughout each month, it is from one to four degrees colder. It certainly is much warmer than our mainland's. These side lands are steep and necessarily difficult of cultivation. My experience does not justify me saying any more on this issue, nor upon the financial side thereof. There are of course many many acres of side lands.

Upon quitting the quarries and proceeding in a northerly direction, as one rose near the table land, and upon same, the East winds were as rushing and biting as ever.

On the morning of the 9th, it was a lovely day, and I sat in the garden of the Villa with the Lessor on the South East side. It was quite warm, and we discussed matters at length. The sudden appearance of *The Gannet* with Trinity Officials decided my leaving then, and by 3pm I was away. In two hours, the Sea and Wind had changed entirely, and I departed with the greatest of difficulty in the Punt, and from thence to the boat which had to be boarded under full sail, because of the heavy Seas. Reaching Instow at 9pm that night, I slept in the Boatman's Cottage.

On the morning of the 10th, I spent a few hours with Capt. Darke, whose 40 years local experience of Lundy ashore, and around same, was material. This is what he says, and he appears a capable man:

1. Lundy will never do any good without any proper landing and embarking facilities.
2. I remember the quarries well. I carried much of the stone, which was sent off in the rough, and dressed at Fremington, where they had Stone Dressing Yards, and then re-boarded for London and elsewhere.
3. The Company's downfall was due to bad management, contracting to supply The Thames Embankment with greater quantities than their output, and at a low price, who bought against the Company, and came on them for the difference. By taking, sending, and quoting on samples from beds near water line (best of material) and sending outcrop stone & having same condemned.
4. Everything was worked by hand, very costly.
5. Shewn the large Ordnance he fixed where the North and east Breakwater Stone Jetties should be, and the Pier, and the reasons therefore. Each Breakwater is 200 yards long, the Pier 100 yards.
6. This, he says, gives first class accommodation for several vessels, any tide, any weather, and many ships would seek same as harbour of refuge and pay £2 per day for such protection.
7. My experience of this work is practically none, and my estimate therefore should not be relied upon. A Civil Engineer with Deep Sea experience should be consulted. He may devise a much cheaper and sounder scheme. To carry out Capt. Darke's ideas, I compute at the lowest will cost Fifty Thousand Pounds(£50,000). I arranged with Capt. Darke, that if I sent for him, and gave him a small consideration for his trouble, he would be pleased to come to Cardiff at any time, this is, if your Lordship would desire.

IN CONCLUSION
1. Granite Quarries will pay (subject to provisos in my report) a company encouraged. (Lessor Royalties and Wharfage).

2. Lundy to be developed; full farming, draining, and re-claiming much Moorland for cultivation. Breeding Cattle, Horses, Sheep, and produce of all kinds to self support 'Greater Lundy', and all stocks. This would pay well on sound lines.
3. Clause 2 is subject is subject to proper landing and embarking facilities being provided, failing which a greater populated and class popular Lundy would never exist.
4. If population (Visitors and Residents) undesired, and landing facilities not entertained, then farming could still be dealt with fully, by Aerial means of Conveyance to ship. Cattle being properly slaughtered on Lundy, and careful handling and suitable boats to receive and discharge.
5. Subject clause 3 being carried out, Hydro Hotel to be built, near The Villa, or Gannets Combe, costing £60,000, to contain 1st class modern conditions, Winter Gardens, Dance Hall, Small Picture House, and a Roulette Hall. The latter in five years should re-pay cost of Hydro, and much of the Harbour and Works. It has no opposition, it can have none, and would attract moneyed attention all over England and Wales. I believe Calais or Dieppe have such a Hall. Run on dignified lines, there can be no harm, no objection, the Government itself are now Co-partners in Race-Horses, as per enclosed cutting. It's a game of Sport. All business contains more or less a spirit of gamble.
6. Suggestion 5, arises out of the alleged rights in my report being legally verified. If Government interference did take place in time, and Roulette abandoned, this Hotel without Licence duties would pay well, and without Excise Duties in addition should yield a great return, and justify your Harbour costs, well.
7. An 18 Hole Golf Course to be put down, and the Old Light-House with slight alterations lends itself for a first rate Pavilion. Rights to graze sheep when not in play over this course to be retained. This would be a great attraction, and would support the Hotel. The Pavilion catering to be run by the Hotel.
8. A large Stores, selling Provisions, and all requisites of life, and of Consumption of Wines and Spirits, and Beers to be established to supply Greater Lundy needs.
9. No outside Trading allowed in any case, and all to pass through Lessor Stores at fair rates would bring in a good return all round.
10. The Bungalow to be the Estate Office.
11. A few Private Police to be appointed, and Lundy to be run with dignity, Law and Order to be well maintained. In Winter, if quiet, Police to be Farm hands.
12. The Lessor's Chief Steward or Manager to reasonable power and discretion for administration, a business man, with technical Building knowledge, for general development and laying out of the Estate, and a Person capable of general control, with dignified advertising.
13. A Doctor to be subsidized until self supporting.
14. A Chemist to be on Store's Staff.

My Lord, my ideas may startle you, but after nearly two months of, may I say, painstaking inquiry and thought, I can come to no other opinion or conclusion.

I trust your Lordship will find time to peruse this Report carefully, and give it your mature consideration, which, to my mind, from financial aspect, it well deserves. The least has been done for Lundy, the most could be.

I have the honour to remain,
Your Lordship's Obedient Servant,
Arthur M. Leon F.I.A.S

[Transcribed from a copy of the original typescript. Only glaring typographical errors have been corrected].

Harman archive

APPENDIX XI

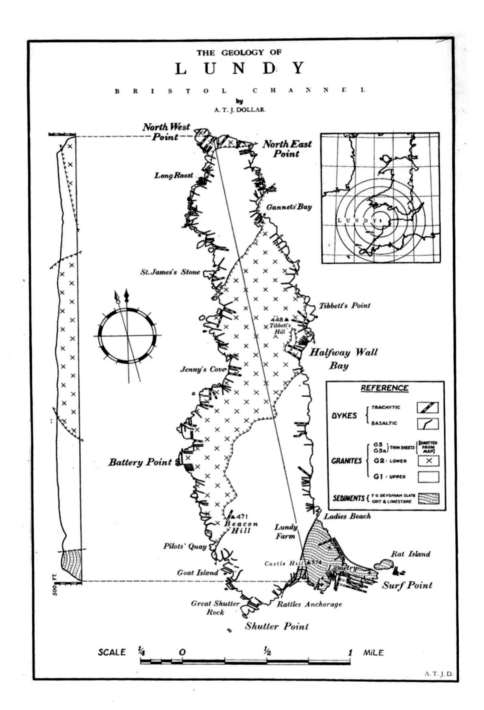

Geology of Lundy - Dr.A.T.J. Dollar - (Ternstrom collection)

APPENDIX XII

An Extract from:-
'Railways and the mid-Victorian income tax.'
The Journal of Transport History, Mar 2003 by Colley, Robert

By adopting a combination of Schedule A and Poor Rate concepts, tax of a substantial amount could be sidestepped. But, more important, the correlation between the profits chargeable to tax and the rewards paid to investors, which was central to the success of the system of deducting tax at source, was eroded. Alerted by the Surveyor's curiosity, the company made a return for 1857 in the slightly increased figure of L(£)35,043, which, although some L30,000 below the figure which Chadwick considered appropriate, was accepted by the General Commissioners. Chadwick applied for a surcharge of L30,000 to be made for the current year, on the grounds that the assessment ought to be equivalent to the amount of rents, dividends and debenture interest from which the company had deducted tax. The appeal by the company against the surcharge is impressive in that the grounds put forward by Baxter concerned exclusively the basis of assessment of railway companies. He contended that the correct basis for tax purposes was the valuation for the Poor Rate, which permitted deductions for depreciation of stock, rails, chairs and sleepers in arriving at the profit of trade assessment. Although he argued the point for almost two hours, no figures were produced to support the returns that had been made. Perhaps, as Cocks remarked about Victorian barristers who dealt with revenue laws, Baxter may not have seen these issues with the same clarity as modern lawyers. He seems not to have addressed, or chose to ignore, the nexus between the profits assessed and the tax retained from rents, dividends and debenture interest. On the other hand, he tested the obvious divergence between the Poor Rate law and revenue law concerning the deductibility of depreciation. Chadwick, reciting the provisions of the taxing statutes, reiterated his opinion that such deductions were prohibited under income tax laws and that the assessment should be at a figure which recouped the tax retained from rents, dividends and debenture interest. The General Commissioners confirmed the surcharge following Chadwick's argument but Baxter's defence was sufficient to absolve the company from any allegation of fraud. Chadwick was advised by the Board to take no further action.

In June 1859 his successor, William Columban M'Kenna, was transferred to Sheffield from Stoke on Trent. M'Kenna, born in mid-Atlantic on a voyage to America, had been sent to England by Daniel O'Connell to seek his fortune; O'Connell had patronage of various kinds and had obtained his nomination for a position in the Board of Stamps and Taxes, a position which was ill suited to M'Kenna's impulsive and restless character and his inherent antagonism to authority. But Surveyors had to be audacious if they were to question the returns of the influential and powerful, and if anyone could take up the cudgels it was the impetuous iconoclast from County Monaghan. M'Kenna inspected the accounts printed for distribution to shareholders and considered the assessments for the years 1854/55 to 1857/58 to be 'notoriously deficient'. His construction of the statute allowed no ambiguity in the rules of Schedule A, and he contended that assessments should be made annually, taking into account the changing level of profitability. It is from his report that the figures in Table 1 were reproduced. The total shortfall in assessment for that period was L140,212 and for the period 1848-53 not less than L150,000. He computed the duty unassessed for the most recent years at L8,315 and for the earlier years at L4,375.

M'Kenna proposed to the Board that he would 'by personal application to one or more of the directors of the company to avoid the necessity of litigation . . . obtain for the Crown the duty which has been so improperly withheld' and wished to do so in a way that would admit of no doubt that it was the Board's intention to enforce the just claims of the Revenue. The Surveyor's powers, however, were fettered by periods of limitation. Often the information came too late. His powers of surcharge had to be exercised either within the time allowed for the commissioners' jurisdiction or within twelve months of the end of the relevant year of assessment, and although he alluded to litigation, the Board's power to prosecute for default in making a true and correct return was similarly restricted. It had to be exercised within two years of the end of the relevant year of assessment. By April 1859 past years of high underassessment were statutorily beyond the reach of the Crown. The Board, tending towards M'Kenna's statutory construction, played with the idea of obtaining the company's consent to a voluntary assessment for the years of underassessment, stressing that the returns had been 'most erroneous' and that tax deducted from rents, dividends and debenture interest payments had been pocketed. But the Board had no power to enforce any measure for the years for which the greatest underassessment had occurred. In the face of resistance offered by the South Yorkshire Railway Company to any suggestion of a voluntary restitution of income tax, the Board was powerless to recover the substantial amounts of duty which had been lost.

It may, however, be simplistic to suppose that the Board was reluctant to prosecute because it was fettered by an impotent law. As Emsley has argued, 'the nineteenth-century state, dependent on a new economic order involving a new level of capitalist investment, a burgeoning factory system and a massive exploitation of coal and iron, would not act against financiers, owners and employers in this new order except when compelled to by the most flagrant abuses'.

What was 'flagrant' was a matter of the discretion of either the Board or the General Commissioners, and that discretion tended to be exercised in favour of the wealthy entrepreneurial elite. Where there was a pause in action, as witnessed in the Board's instructions to both Chadwick and M'Kenna to take no further action, it may have been intended in order that the period of limitation for the earlier year could expire. When it could still legally have instituted proceedings for some of the earlier years, there is a noticeable reluctance on its part to move beyond the current year. The correspondence exhibits a Fabian quality which is the antithesis of the urgency so apparent in cases of individual and smaller taxpayers Was this simply tactical, in the sense that while the possibility of some substantial restitution of duty remained, that would far exceed any potential penalty, the Board was prepared to abrogate its capacity to prosecute? Or was it symptomatic of a more complex attitude to persons of standing and substance, when they came into conflict with the Board, by which they were treated with special courtesy and regard? Did those who exercised the discretion of the Board deal in a special way with the entrepreneurial elite who played such a critical role in the expansion of a transport system that would benefit trade both at home and for export?

Such personal prejudices are almost impossible to ascertain with certainty, but it is probable that, beyond the formal relationship between the railway company and the Surveyor, there were other layers of communication, where agreements were reached and informal arrangements made, and which took place outside the official arena of assessment and appeal. The Surveyor at the front rank of tax assessment may have been outgeneralled by a small but active body of higher civil servants and interested industrialists. Certainly in the South Yorkshire Railway case the directors and Secretary of the company had meetings with the Revenue solicitor at which it was informally agreed that the Board would not pursue the matter of underassessment beyond the current year, though the reasons were not recorded.

APPENDIX XIII

The text of a statement issued by Samual Griffiths regarding the Election of 1865 in the Borough of Wolverhampton with refernces to Philip Vanderbyl.

TO THE ELECTORS
OF THE BOROUGH OF
WOLVERHAMPTON.
GENTLEMEN,

A certain 'clique' in the Borough of Wolverhampton known as the Walker party, has been very industrious during the last fourteen days in circulating the report that there would be no contest for the Borough, and has induced 'the Post,' 'the Gazette,' and the 'Wolverhampton Chronicle,' to give publicity to this Statement, which everyone knows is the parent of their own most ardent wishes.

Their friend, Mr. Weguelin, they say will not be opposed. So far so good. To this statement I take no exception. Last week, however, this same Walker party got hold of the correspondent of the 'Daily Post,' and among other things induced him to state in that paper in respect to Philip Vanderbyl, Esq., (director of the National Bank, a member of the eminent firm of Redfern Alexander and Company, and without exception, one of the most wealthy, able, and influential merchants in London, and who supplies more orders for iron for these districts, than any man I know in London), that he belonged to a tory family, ergo, he was a tory. Now I have to state which I do hereby aver as a gentleman, that Mr. Philip Vanderbyl is a liberal, of the school of the great Gladstone and that he does not belong to a Tory family.

I find in this day's 'Post' it is stated that it is my intention to offer myself as a candidate and be nominated on the Hustings, with the view of making a speech and then retiring from the contest.

This wicked imputation on my character as a political man is too contemptible for a contradiction, suffice it to say, that if I permit my hearty supporters to nominate me for this Election, the efforts of myself and friends will increase in vigour until the electoral urn is closed by the Mayor on the day of the election, and no legitimate means will be spared to defeat a wretched Oligarchy, and by the results of the election crown the temple of freedom of one of the most disinterested, educated, and independent constituencies in the United Kingdom.

ELECTORS OF THE BOROUGH OF WOLVERHAMPTON,

Wait! I have not offered myself to the constituency at present, for this election -- I decline to say what I MAY do, in respect to soliciting your suffrages --- let me offer very heartily my most sincere thanks to the Nine Hundred Independent Electors who voted for me at the last election, and be assured that I am still and ever shall remain grateful.

With regard to Mr. PHILIP VANDERBYL, I may inform you that, notwithstanding his extensive connection with this Borough in a business point of view, he has positively declined to solicit your suffrages during this present election.

I remain, Gentlemen,
Yours Faithfully,
SAMl. GRIFFITHS,

Whitmore Reans Hall,
Wolverhampton, July 5th. 1865

APPENDIX XIV

An interview with Tim Marsh, from the Lundy Island Chronicle, Spring 1983.

Tim is a 'banker' mason or stone cutter: 'Granite differs from site to site and is defined by the fineness of its grain...most of Lundy's granite tends towards the rough end of the spectrum although the biggest quarry has fine grained granite.. [it] is much harder to cut, but cuts much cleaner.

Good quality granite is described as 'blue granite'. Brown granite or 'list' is found at the edges of fissures in the granite where seeping water has stained the stone. 'Elvin' is the name of the grey stripe planning through some granite, 'lamb's leg' is another name for it. Samples of all these may be found on Lundy.

When starting a quarry the first things to look for are the natural joints or faults coming down vertically. These are called the 'tough way' joints and the 'cleaving way'. In theory a piece of granite should come out cleanly if it is cut along the 'quartering way', which is 90 degrees to the tough way joint.

...The Lundy quarries are not easy to work because there are so many tough way joints and it's quite difficult to get a good long piece of granite...The pieces of granite would have been hauled out from the quarry by means of cranes sited usually at the corners and/or above each quarry. The bases on which the cranes on Lundy were fixed can still be seen in each of the quarries.'

APPENDIX XV

Significant Dates Relating to Quarrying on Lundy.

10 July 1863 - Agreement drawn up between W. C. McKenna and J. N. McKenna regarding the transfer of lease and rights to proposed LGC.
18 July 1863 - Lundy Granite Co. Ltd. registered.
15 August 1863 - Lease granted to W. C. McKenna.
19 November 1868 - The winding-up of the LGC ordered by the court.
19 February 1869 - Whiffen appointed liquidator.
22 July 1875 - LGC finally dissolved by order of the Court.
8 December 1896 - Lease granted to Charles Pinn who later claimed there had been an agreement to defer payment of rents until the quarries were productive. Charles Pinn was contractor from Exeter who had been on Lundy working on the church.
15 December 1897 - Lundy Granite Quarries Ltd. registered. Formed to take over Pinn's lease for £5, 800 as £4,600 in shares and cash for setting up expenses for the new company. The deal was not completed.
1898 - Property Securities Syndicate Ltd. registered.
9 December 1899 - Incorporation of Lundy Island & Mainland Quarries Ltd.
26 October 1900 - The winding-up of the Lundy Granite Quarries Ltd. The lease had been mortgaged to the Property Securities Co Ltd., who agreed to sell it to the Industrial Debenture Co. Ltd, who were to assign the lease in Dec **1899** - to The Lundy Granite Quarries Ltd. The deal was not implemented as the Company did not go to allotment.
1901 - Lease assigned by Pinn to Property Securities Co. Ltd
9 April 1902 - Lundy Island & Mainland Quarries Ltd. purchases the lease from Property Securities Co. Ltd.
26 May 1902 -Lundy Island & Mainland Quarries Ltd. registered.
1906 - Lease withdrawn by H. G. Heaven as the Island was put up for sale.
11 June 1907 - Lundy Island & Mainland Quarries Ltd amalgamated with Property Securities Co Ltd.
10 February 1911 - Lundy Island & Mainland Quarries Ltd dissolved.
20 March 1916 - Arthur Leon's report to Baron Rhondda, a prospective purchaser.
January 1922 - George Beaufort Richards's report to Mr. A. L. Christie.
1998 - Lundy Quarry Complex scheduled as an Ancient Monument.

ACKNOWLEDGMENTS

Thanks are due to:-
The Lundy Field Society for their permission to use material originally published in 'Lundy -The Quarry Complex: Some Notes, Observations and Speculations.' *Lundy Field Society Report,* 1999, No. 50, pp 70-93, by Peter Rothwell.
The Devonshire Association for their consent to the use of
material originally published in 'Granite: A Failed Enterprise on Lundy, 1864-1869,' *Transactions of the Devonshire Association,* 2005, No. 137, pp 193-219, by M. Ternstrom.
The National Archive for permission to use material relating to quarrying on Lundy, and Company documents.
The National Monuments Record for permission to use aerial photographs of Lundy.

We are grateful to the following friends for their help in writing and assembling this book:

Tom Baker, for the loan of granite company share certificates.

Andrew Burke of Slee Blackwell, for providing legal transcript and analysis.

Dr. Robert Colley, for permission to quote from his paper.

Tony Cutler, for reading and discussing the MS.

Jeff Evans for copies of extracts from The Times.

Members of the Heaven family for access to their archive and permission to use photographs.

Diana Keast, for the loan of papers from the Harman Archive.

Reg Lo-Vel, for the loan of the Lundy Granite Company's prospectus, 1863.

Alan Rowland, for loan of Frederick Wilkins' letterhead.

Derek Sach, for his collection of photographs.

Peter Stanier, for reading and commenting on the original text.

Colin Taylor, forpermission to use his plan.

Caroline Thackray, National Trust Archaeological Unit, for copies of the surveys made of the quarries.

Ann Westcott, for her steadfast support of the project, for proofing the manuscript and so much more.

REFERENCES & BIBLIOGRAPHY

The Barnstaple Times, 8 June 1869

The Bideford Gazette, 15 May 1866; 3 July 1866

Bouquet, M., 1862, 'Lundy Granite Boom,' *Western Morning News,* 3 September

Chanter, J. R., 1877, *Lundy Island,* Reprinted 1997

Colley, M., 'Railways & the Mid-Victorian Income Tax,'
    The Journal of Transport History, March 2003.

Dollar, A. T. J., 'The Lundy Complex: Petrology & Tectonics,'
    Quarterly Journal of the Geological Society, xcvii, pp 38-77

Dunning, M., *Devon Churches,* 2001, Francis Frith

Exeter Flying Post, 15 March 1871, 6 March 1872, 27 March 1872

Harman Archive, private collection

Heaven Archive, private collection

Hemming, G. W., *Law Reports, Chancery: Appeal Cases,* vi, 1870-1871

The Home Friend, Nos 47 - 58, 1853

Hoskins, W., *Devon,* 1992

Irving, R.A., Schofield A.J., Webster, C.A., Eds: *Island Studies,* 1997,
    Lundy Field Society

Langham, A. F., *The Island of Lundy,* 1994

Larn, R., *Devon Shipwrecks,* 1974

Larn R., & Larn, B., *Shipwreck Index of the British Isles,* 1995, Lloyds.

L'Estrange, The Revd A. G., *Yachting Round the West of England,* 1965

The Mining Journal, 11 August 1866, p. 509

National Archives: Legal proceedings following the dissolution of the
                     Lundy Granite Company.
                     Full references are given in Ternstrom, 2005

National Trust Archive, London S.W.1.

National Monuments Record, Swindon.

*North Devon Journal,*31 March 1864; 20 August 1868; 18 January 1869
           25 February 1869; 21 July 1870; 3 August 1871; 6 June 1872.

North Devon Record Office, Barnstaple.
        'North Devon 50 years Ago', D. O. 040

Rothwell, P., 'Lundy - The Quarry Complex: Some Notes, Observations, and
        Speculations,' *Lundy Field Society Report*, 50, 1999, pp 70-81

Slattery, Sir Matthew, 'Troubled Times,' *The Three Banks Review*, 1972.

Smith S., & Roberts, C., 'The Geology of Lundy,' *Island Studies*, 1977, pp 59-66

Smitz, C. J. 'The Granite Quarries and Mineral Mines of Lundy,'
        Bristol Archaeological Society Journal, 10, 1977, pp 23-26

Stanier, P., 'The Granite Quarrying Industry in Devon & Cornwall' 1800-1910,
        The Industrial Archaeology Review, 1985, Vol 7, Part 2, pp 171-189

        South West Granite, 1999, Cornish Hillside Publications

Ternstsrom, M., 'Granite: A Failed Enterprise on Lundy,' 2005,
        Transactions of the Devonshire Assn., 137, pp. 193-220

Trinity House archive, Guildhall Library, London.

INDEX

A
Aberdeen 137, 160
Accommodation 15, 27, 116, 124, 157
 blocks 35, 41, 106
Accountant 35, 85, 127-8
Act 59, 86, 98, 104, 116, 125, 127-8, 132, 143-6, 148, 172
Act of Parliament 108, 143
Adit 16
Admiralty 20, 89
Advertisement 15, 23, 26, 93, 96
Aerial Cable-way 162
Aerial view of Main Platform and Lower Inclines 6
Aerial Conveyor 166
Agents 43, 85, 98, 115-6, 118, 120-1, 133
AGM 83, 86
Agreement 19, 26-7, 94-7, 99, 100, 125, 132, 147, 173, 176
Alterations 41, 168
Appeal 100, 103, 144-5, 148, 171, 173
Applicant 143-4
Application 86-8, 114, 136-7, 143-5
Arable lands 97, 122, 132
Arbitration 117, 121, 126-8
Arbitrators 127-8
Area, reserved 6, 18, 20, 29
Arrangement 19, 26, 46, 109-10, 120, 146, 156
Arthur M. Leon 169
Articles of Association 86, 103
Asquith 20
Assessments 14, 119, 171-3
Assets 93, 100-2, 106, 112-3, 140
Auction 87-8, 94, 101-2

B
Bankers 29, 31, 53, 109
Barnstaple 142
Barnstaple County Court 135
Barnstaple Times 87, 102, 178
Baron Rhondda of Llanwern 63, 109, 112, 164, 176
Barton Cottages 22
Basalt Elvan 164
Base-blocks 74-5
Base-plates 75
Baxter 171
Beach 15, 46, 63, 67, 74-5, 81, 84, 99, 123
Beach 77
Benthall, Henry 93-103, 113-4, 131-3, 140-1, 145
Bideford 12, 84, 86, 99, 102, 104, 141
Blocks 35, 47, 67, 74-5, 106, 138, 141, 154, 156, 158, 165
Board 19, 59, 85, 123-4, 141
 of Directors 109
 of Stamps and Taxes 19, 171
 of Works 26

Boats 20, 75, 123, 166-8
Bolts 51, 74-5
Borers 6, 36-7
Borough of Wolverhampton 112, 174
Brake drums 7, 46, 58-9, 61
Breakwater 16, 116, 119, 156, 166-7
Bridgwater 83, 94, 114
Bristol 13, 16, 97, 129-32, 135
Bristol Channel 11-3, 115, 160
Bristol Dock Committee 160
Brogden, John & Alexander 85
Bronze Age 6, 11
Bubble companies 87
Buckland wood houses 20
Builders 11, 15, 29, 81, 99, 101, 160
Buildings 6, 15, 35, 41, 54, 75, 81, 87-8, 98, 106, 109, 115-9, 121, 123, 125-7, 137
Buyer 16, 90, 93

C
Cables 46-7, 59, 63
Cableway 63
Calves 88
Cape, George 86, 89, 113-4
Capital 15, 23, 26-7, 84, 106, 114, 155, 161, 166
 paid-up 156
Capt. Darke 167
Captain 131, 134-5
Cardiff 90, 167
Cargo 83, 97-8, 103, 131-3
Caroline 85
Caroline Helps Morris 115, 119, 125, 128
Carriage 14, 89
Case 85, 94, 117, 124-5, 127, 144-5
Cash 96, 98, 103, 133, 176
Castle 20
 keep 6, 21
Catholics 108
Cattle 87, 90, 122, 168
Certificate 160-1
Chadwick 171-2
Chain 47, 59, 140
Chancery 101, 178
Chanter 67, 178, 180
Chanter's map 7, 67, 69
Chapels 98, 115-6
Charges 15, 86-7, 90, 102, 109, 120-1, 128
Chatham 89
Chief Clerk 136
Church 13, 99, 106, 119, 134, 137-8, 176
Church of England 98, 103, 108, 116
Class 108, 155-7, 168
 entrepreneurial 108
Claxton, Capt. 91
Cliffs 12, 20, 27, 63, 67, 81, 157
Clock 88, 134

Clovelly 67
Clover 122
Coal 35, 83, 85, 123, 135, 172
Commission 93, 96
Committee 15, 129, 135
Compactness 157
Company
  AGM 83
  assets 94, 100
  directors 94
  documents 177
  effects 94
  employees 75
  officers 29
  personnel 104
  secretary 86
  ships 106
Company's accounts 89
Company's employees 137
Comparative plans 30
Compensation 116-7, 122, 127-8, 147
Compost 122
Construction 7, 13, 46, 51, 63, 69, 75, 106, 119, 127, 154-5, 160, 162, 171
Contract 23, 26-7, 83, 86, 89, 90, 93-4, 100, 113
Convict labour 16
Copper 15, 41, 164
Cornish Granite 166
Cornish Quarries 157
Cornish and Scottish granite 63
Cornwall 13, 51, 67, 162, 164
Costelloe, Francis 85, 89, 113
Cottages 6, 20-1, 27, 29, 35, 41, 98, 103, 106, 135, 137, 166
Cottages, Barton 6, 22, 35, 137
Council 127-8
Counter-weight 46
Court 5, 86, 89, 90, 93, 96, 99-101, 103, 106, 114, 128, 135, 137, 143-8, 176
  orders 100, 104, 113
  proceedings 6, 47
Court of Appeal 148
Covenants 93, 95, 115, 122, 125-6, 128
Crane 67, 101-2, 175
  base 51
Credit 93, 109
Creditors 90, 100, 144-8
  company's 103
Crew 35, 85, 123
Crops 83, 126-7
Crown 13, 172
Cultivation 20, 126, 167-8

D
Dagenham Docks 83
Dartmoor Granite Company 26, 94
Dead Rent 160
Debt 16, 83, 86-7, 89, 90, 94, 97, 100, 143-4, 147
  company's 86, 103

Deeds 125, 127
Deficiencies in Assets on Lundy 112
Deposits 16, 89, 127, 134
Depot 26, 83, 87-8, 94, 113-4, 155
Depreciation 102, 171
Derricks 67, 81
Devon 2, 13, 51, 88, 117, 124, 137-8, 178
Directors 19, 20, 23, 26-7, 81, 83-7, 89-91, 93, 103, 109-10, 113-4, 134, 161, 172-4
Distrain 100, 143-4, 146-8
Dividends 86, 156, 162, 171-2
Dockyards 16, 160
Dollar, Dr A. T. J. 13, 170, 178
Drills 36-7
Dung 122
Duty 172

E
Easements 115, 117-8
Election 94, 112, 114, 174
Elite, entrepreneurial 172
Eliza 141-2
Employees 35, 85-6, 135
Endellion 139
Engineers 35, 69, 81, 85-6, 101, 109, 160, 162
Engines 121
English law 144
Enterprise 16, 46, 51, 101, 109-10
Equipment 35, 43, 53, 67, 81
Erections 117, 121, 123, 162
Establishment 26, 29, 43, 81, 94, 108, 114, 157
Estate 15, 97, 128, 131, 143, 146-7, 168
Etheridge, Robert 157
Evidence 11, 35, 41, 43, 46-7, 51, 53, 59, 62-3, 67, 75, 103, 110, 122, 127, 135
Ex parte Heaven 143
Excursion to Lundy Island 20
Expenditure 15, 83, 97, 122, 132, 161, 164-5
Expenses 15, 20, 62, 83, 86, 90, 99, 103, 116, 122-3, 126, 128-31, 157, 161, 176
Expiration 115, 126, 128
Extracts 112, 115, 120, 137, 160, 164, 171, 177

F
Falmouth 129-30
Farm 6, 13, 15, 20, 23, 29, 87, 90, 95-8, 101, 103-4, 109, 113, 116, 124, 156
  buildings 29
Farmhands 86
Farmhouse 6, 14, 20, 29, 31, 87, 93, 121, 125-6
Farming 85, 116, 126, 168
  stock 87-8, 96-7, 127, 131
Fees 27, 103, 115, 128
Fences 121-2, 125
Finances, company's 26
Fittings 75, 87-8
Fodder 20, 86, 90, 122
Fog signal station 13, 20
Forge 35

Foundation blocks 7, 67
Freight 142, 155-7, 166
Fremington 26, 83, 86-8, 90, 101, 103, 113, 141, 167
  depot 26
Fremington Quay 6, 25, 69, 102
Fuel 123
Furness 26

G
Gade, Felix 31, 43
Gannet 167
Gannet's Bay 46
Gannet's Combe 116, 124, 168
Gardens 29, 35, 41, 117, 167
Gates 29, 121, 125
General Commissioners 171-2
Geology of Lundy 170, 179
Gi's Hut 43
Gladstone 174
Golden Square 29, 137
Goods 29, 46, 87, 97-8, 102, 116, 123, 131, 133, 143-8, 160
Gould 142, 157
Government House 41
Granite
  blocks 6, 29, 37, 69, 81, 106
    dressed 81
  boulders 67, 74
  coarse-grained megacrystic 13
  columns 53, 79, 81
  crushed 160
  facings 99
  finer-grained megacrystic 13
  finished 53
  mass 13, 154
  outcrops 51
  porphyry 115-21, 125
  quarries 20, 23, 27, 31, 63, 113, 138, 154, 161-2, 164, 167
  quays 67
  sand 75
  sleepers 6, 51
  specimens of 23, 154
  steps 41, 59
  undressed 106
  works 26, 84, 106, 114, 131, 164
Granite Company graves 136

H
Hand-borers 36
Harbour 116, 119, 124, 156, 160, 167-8
Harbour 23
Harbour of refuge 167
Harbour of Refuge 16, 160
Harbours 67
Harman Archive 14, 135-8, 169,177-8
Harman VC, John Pennington 106
Hartland Quay 69
Haven, Milford 85

Haytor Granite Company 158
Head 23, 46-7, 51, 59, 63, 158
Heard, William 31, 35, 43-4, 51
Heaven
  Cecilia 75
  family 15, 20, 29, 41, 106, 177
Heaven Archive 12, 14-5, 17-8, 21, 28, 31, 48, 75, 82, 85, 92, 96, 178
Heaven Family 5, 6, 12
Heaven family outing 7, 82
Henry Sothan 20
Highbridge 26, 69, 83, 90, 94, 113-4
His Majesty's Courts, 128, 137
Holes 74-5
  drill 81
Home Rule Party 19
Horses 31, 53, 85, 87-8, 168
Hospital 6, 35, 38, 43, 46, 106, 137
Hotel 168
Houses 29, 83, 87-8, 117-8, 123, 125-6, 146
  dwelling 117, 123
Howard's Quarry 51, 83, 140

I
Ilfracombe 12, 67, 102, 131, 134, 160, 164
Incline 46
  1 46
  2 46-7
  3 46-7
  single-track 43, 46
  twin-track 43, 46
  upper 5, 43
    lower 6, 33
Income 15-6, 20, 95, 103, 106, 108
  tax 165-6, 172
Indenture 128
Infrastructure 43, 81, 109
Inhabitants 27, 29, 135
Injunctions 100
Inspection 121, 157, 162, 164
Instow 20, 155, 167
Interest 84, 93, 95, 99, 100, 110, 126, 127, 139, 155-6, 180
International Exhibition 16, 23
Iron 94, 101, 125-6, 140, 172, 174
  rails 59, 81
  sockets 7, 75, 77
  staples 7
Iron Buildings 101, 166
Island
  plateau 15, 29, 35, 51
  use 97, 131
Islanders 75, 136

J
Jetty
  foundation blocks 81
  wooden 31
Jetty base block 7, 76-7

Joint-stock companies 87, 109
Judge Sarjeant Petersdorff 135
Judgement 5, 100, 162

K
Keep 6
Kenna 171-2
Kerb-stones 81
Kohima 106
Kyffin Freeman 162

L
Labour 15, 29, 91, 97-8, 102, 131-3
Lambs 141
Land 75, 86, 115-8, 121-3, 125, 127, 135-6, 143-4, 146-8, 156
Landing 3, 12, 15, 20, 116, 141
Landing bay 3, 12, 15, 20, 29, 84, 116, 141
Landing Beach 6, 12, 46, 48, 51, 81, 85
Landlord 20, 100, 110, 119, 121, 143-7
Langham 35, 46-7, 59, 178, 180
Larn 178
Lease 15, 16, 19, 20, 21, 46, 52, 67, 93-100, 103, 106,
Lease 46, 126
Legislature 147
Leon
  Arthur 63
  Arthur M. 164
Lessee 16, 19, 20, 26, 95, 100, 143-7, 156
Lessor 94, 145-8, 160, 167
Letter 15, 75, 90-1, 97, 121, 127, 129-30, 132
The Liberator 19
Lighthouse 6, 20, 28, 115, 135, 162
Lime 123, 125-6
Limestone 123
Lintels 35, 41, 81
Liquidation 51, 87-8, 95, 100-1, 147-8
Liquidator 86, 87, 89, 90, 93, 99-104, 113-4, 137, 147-8
Litigation 172
Livestock 86, 88, 94, 102, 126
Load 23, 131, 138, 141, 158
London 23, 26, 86, 91, 94, 99, 129-30, 155-6, 162, 167, 174, 178-9
  granite company 20
Lord Romilly 7, 143, 147-8
Losses 83-4, 86, 89, 102
Lundy Roads 12, 20, 85, 131

M
Machinery 35, 47, 83, 87-8, 90, 95, 101-2, 104, 115-6, 121, 126, 162, 165-6
Main Incline 5, 7, 43, 46-7, 59, 63, 68, 70
  top of 7, 58, 60-1
Main Platform 5, 6, 29, 31, 33, 43, 46-7, 49-51, 53, 59
Main tramway 6, 7, 43, 49, 51, 54-5
Mainland 26, 31, 51, 87, 135, 162, 167
  granite quarries 51
  quarries 161

Management 15, 63, 90, 98, 123, 129, 155
Manager 29, 35, 41, 89, 93, 114, 137, 162, 168
  of quarries 104
Mangel worzel 122
Map 6, 32, 67, 155, 180
Market 15, 27, 84, 90, 97, 131-2, 157, 166
Marks 6, 36-7, 42, 51
  bolt 74
  sleeper 6, 7, 55
Masonry 7, 46-7, 60, 63, 137
Masons 11, 53, 69, 81, 109, 134, 156, 162
Mast-crane 51, 75, 81
Master of the Rolls 7, 86, 89, 102, 144-5
Materials 43, 51, 63, 87-8, 99, 106, 119-20, 157, 166-7, 177
McKenna 91, 93-5, 97-8, 100, 109, 112, 115, 132-3, 140, 144-5, 147, 176
  Edward 26, 93, 101, 103, 140
  Joseph 19, 26, 85, 108-10
  Michael 19
    Reginald 20
  William 16, 19, 20, 93-5, 98, 101, 114
Mechanism 47, 59
Meeting room 29
Members 6, 12, 26, 85, 108-9, 148, 174, 177
Mersey Docks and Harbour Board 160
Messuages 116, 119, 123, 126
Metropolitan Board of Works 26
Middle Quarry 7, 51, 83, 107, 140
Midland Bank 20
Millcombe 6, 14
Millcombe Valley 15, 20
Minerals 13, 15-6, 116-7, 164
Mines 116-7
M'Kennna 171-2
Money 86, 89, 90, 96-7, 103, 109, 128, 131-2
Monies 128, 147, 156
Moorstone Granite 129
Moorstones 11
Mortgage 16, 95, 99, 114, 128
MP 26, 109, 113-4
Mr. Harman 31
Muck 122
Murray, Adam 130

N
National Archives 51, 105, 111, 134, 136-7, 177-8
National Bank 7, 19, 26, 83-7, 89, 90, 93, 97, 109, 113, 134, 174
National Trust 13, 63, 81, 110
Negotiations 26, 98, 145
Nominees 83-6, 97
Nonconformist 108
North Devon Journal Herald 84, 136
North and South Lights 63
Norton, John 138

O
O'Connell, Daniel 19, 171
Officers 29, 81, 90, 97, 135
Official liquidator 87-9, 102, 114, 145-7
Officials, company 41
Ogmore 95, 136
Old Broad Street 7, 93
Old Light-House 168
Orders, winding-up 89, 143-4
Ordnance Survey 7, 43, 46, 59, 63, 67, 77
  map 32, 41, 70
  of Lundy 6
Outline of Quarry Quay 67, 69, 71
Output 161, 165-7
Owner 11, 13, 95, 106, 113, 135, 138, 172

P
Parliament 108, 143, 148
Path 29, 31, 41, 43, 118
Payment 26, 52, 84, 89, 93, 97, 100, 103, 106, 117, 119, 123, 125, 128, 132, 156-7
  initial 26
Permission 2, 124, 137, 177
Petitions 87, 89
Philadelphia 19
Pier 7, 14, 20, 77, 114, 116, 119, 129, 160, 162, 167
Pigs 29, 87-8
Pinn, Charles 176
Pitches 164
Plaintiff 91
Plans 6
Plant 14-5, 83-4, 87-8, 90, 95, 101-2, 113, 117, 121, 166
Plateau 43, 46, 51, 138
Platform 29, 31, 35, 43, 47, 63
Plugs & feathers 37
Plymouth 131
Police 135, 168
Poor Rate 171
Porphyry 115-126, 164
Ports 23, 67, 138, 155, 158
Possession 20, 86, 93, 95-6, 100-2, 113, 145-6, 156, 161
Posts 113-4, 120, 124-5, 174
Powder magazine 6, 51, 54
Powers 19, 86, 108, 115-9, 121-3, 128, 144-7, 168, 172
Premises 87, 89, 94, 103, 118, 121-2, 124-8
Price 103, 124, 127, 131-2, 135-6, 146, 155, 157, 162
  average 155-6
Privileges 109, 115, 117-8, 122, 156
Profits 13, 23, 100-1, 103, 142, 155-6, 161, 165, 171
Properties of Lundy Granite 157
Property 13, 41, 87-8, 95, 100, 116, 121, 143-6, 162
Property Securities Co Ltd 176
Proprietor 20, 143
Prospectus 19, 23, 63, 112, 154, 160
Provisos 119, 126, 167

Public works 11, 156
Pulley wheel 47
Pump House 35-6, 41
Purchase 13, 16, 19, 83-4, 87-8, 99, 102-3, 134, 176
  money 93, 95, 100, 114
Purchasers 16, 102

Q
Quarries
  main 5, 51
  middle 51
  northernmost 51
  test 51
  upper 138
Quarry Beach 7, 31, 46, 53, 66, 67, 69, 75, 77-8, 81
Quarry Buildings 6, 34
Quarry Complex 7, 56, 177, 179
Quarry Cottages 5, 6, 35-6, 39-41, 43, 53, 106
Quarry manager's cottage 41
Quarry Pond 36, 43
Quarrying rights 11, 109
Quarrymen 29, 35-6, 86, 109
Quartz 164
Quay 14, 31, 43, 46, 59, 63, 67, 69, 74-5, 81, 116, 123, 129

R
Rails 23, 62, 67, 81, 121, 158, 171
Ratchet Steps 7, 58, 60
River Taw 69
Roadstone 163-4
Royal Commission 94, 114

S
Sand, silver 75
School-room 116
Schneider, Charles John 140
Sea View 29
Share
  capital 16, 23
  certificate 6, 25
      Issue 6
Sheep 87, 90, 101, 141, 168
Sideland 29, 43, 46-7, 51-2, 63
Silver 15
Sir Joseph McKenna 86
Sleepers 42, 54, 171
Slipway 6
Smith#s Point Quarry 140
South Monaghan 19
St. Helen's Church 6, 30, 138
St. Helen's Field 22
Stacey Estate 164
Staples 7, 73
Stores 168
Surveyor of Taxes 19
Swansea 160
Swell jumpers 36

T
Tavern & Stores 4, 22, 104
Taylor, Robt. H 161
Thomas, George 135
Tie-bar 59, 64
Timber piles 75
Time-check Platform 5, 31, 43, 45
The Times 23, 85
Tools 36, 83, 95, 101-2, 131, 161, 165
  quarrymen's 36, 53
Torridge 99
Track 47
Trickett, Samuel 158
Trinity House 15, 179
Trinity Officials 167
Trolley wheels 7, 55

V
Vanderbyl, Philip 83, 94, 114, 134-5
Vanderbyl 26, 35, 84, 90, 93, 113, 141
VC 106-7
Vessels 46, 74-5, 85, 91, 97, 123-4, 131-2, 154-5, 167
Villa 6, 14-5, 20, 29, 167-8
Village 6, 27, 28-30

W
Waste tips 51, 162
Well-head 36
Westward Ho! 99
Wharfage 167
Whiffin, George 86-8, 102, 112, 114
Wilkins 86, 97-8, 101, 131, 133, 136
William Heards Quarry 6, 44, 51
Williams, George 115, 119, 125
Window-sills 81
Woody Bay Pier 7, 77
Workings 35, 46, 51, 81, 106, 138, 164
Works 26
Wrought-iron 7, 80

Y
Youghal 19

Z
Zig-zag terraces 66, 68

THE AUTHORS

Peter Rothwell has been fascinated by Lundy and its history since his first visit to the island on August the 18th 1958, eight days after his eleventh birthday (as  he proudly recorded in green Biro on the map in the back of Richard Perry's *'Lundy, Isle of Puffins'* - 1959's visit was recorded in red Biro!). Since that occasion he has visited many times and has published a visual celebration of the island in *'Lundy - an Island Sketchbook'* and also illustrated the reprint of *'Lundy Island, A Monograph'* by J. R. Chanter, both published by Westwell Publishing. Peter has been researching the history of commercial quarrying on Lundy for a number of years and this book is the culmination of those studies. He is tutor on the sketching courses organised by Westwell on the island each summer.

Myrtle Ternstrom (formerly Langham) first went to Lundy in 1952 and has visited it regularly ever since. Her particular interest is in the island's history, and research is ongoing. She was part-author with Tony Langham of two books about the island, and since then has published a number of others, as well as being joint editor and publisher of F. W. Gade's Memoir, *'My Life on Lundy.'* Her enjoyment of Lundy arises from its tranquillity, the clear air, the wind, the sea and the birdsong; the friends she has made there, and the fact that it is an engrossing and yet encompassable subject of study. In 1999 Lundy's development, with consideration of comparable small islands, was the subject of her doctoral thesis. She is recognised as the principal authority on the island's history.